NEW IN CHESS bestsellers

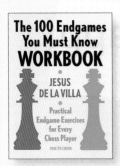

The 100 Endgames You Must Know Workbook
Practical Endgames Exercises for Every Chess Player
Jesus de la Villa 288 pages - €22.95

"I love this book! In order to master endgame principles you will need to practice them."
NM Han Schut, Chess.com

"The perfect supplement to De la Villa's manual. To gain sufficient knowledge of theoretical endgames you really only need two books."
IM Herman Grooten, Schaaksite

1001 Chess Exercises for Club Players
The Tactics Workbook that Also Explains All Key Concepts
Frank Erwich 192 pages - €17.95

"Good work! Lots of exercises, not many words, just what I like. The chapter on defence, in particular, is very cleverly done. One is so accustomed to attacking combinations, but tactics can be used in defence as well."
GM Simen Agdestein, VG Daily News

"I was very impressed by the range of positions that Erwich selected." – *GM Matthew Sadler*

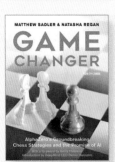

How Ulf Beats Black
Ulf Andersson's Bulletproof Strategic Repertoire for White
Cyrus Lakdawala 288 pages - €27.95

This repertoire will last a lifetime.

"There is a lot of good stuff to enjoy by exploring the ideas and openings of the Swedish legend."
IM Gary Lane, ECF Newsletter

"Lakdawala has come up with a 'not the usual fare, but definitely worth the detour' type of work. It's instructive, but not too heavy, so will suit all sorts."
GM Glenn Flear, Yearbook 127

The Agile London System
A Solid but Dynamic Chess Opening Choice for White
Alfonso Romero & Oscar de Prado 336 pages - €26.95

Reveals the secrets behind sharp ideas such as the Barry Attack, the Jobava Attack and the hyper-aggressive Pereyra Attack.

"With plenty of fresh material that should ensure that it will be the reference work on the complete London System for years to come." – *GM Glenn Flear*

"Encyclopedic in scope." – *John Hartmann, ChessLife*

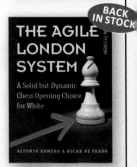

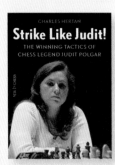

Game Changer
AlphaZero's Groundbreaking Chess Strategies and the Promise of AI
Matthew Sadler & Natasha Regan 416 pages - €22.50

"Every chess player should have this book."
IM Malcolm Pein

"Once you experience the power of these ideas in your own game, you realise how much we can learn from the playing style of AlphaZero." – *IM Stefan Kuipers*

"I love it. This is a phenomenal book."
IM John Bartholomew

Devoted to Chess
The Creative Heritage of Yuri Razuvaev
Compiled by **Boris Postovsky** 368 pages - €29.95

Yuri Razuvaev (1945-2012) was a leading Soviet GM, a first-rate chess author and a world-class trainer. He worked with Karpov, Kramnik, Gelfand, Lautier, Salov, Topalov, Kosteniuk, Carlsen, Caruana and many others.

"Studying the creative heritage of Yuri Razuvaev will bring you great benefits" – *Vladimir Kramnik*

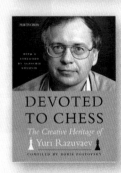

Strike like Judit!
The Winning Tactics of Chess Legend Judit Polgar
Charles Hertan 256 pages - €24.95

"Thanks to Hertan's well-written explanations, the reader too should be able to increase their own killer instinct."
CHESS Magazine (UK)

"Judit was a superb tactician, and the book collects her finest combinations."
GM Simen Agdestein, VG Daily Newspaper (Norway)

Techniques of Positional Play
45 Practical Methods to Gain the Upper Hand in Chess
Valeri Bronznik & Anatoli Terekhin 254 pages - €24.95

"One of the best books on positional play you're ever likely to read." – *Paul Kane Manchester Chess Federation*

"I am absolutely convinced that every (really every!) chess player will learn a whole lot from this book. For me personally it is one of the best chess books on the market today."
Martin Rieger, Schachwelt

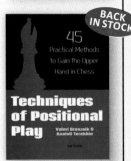

The New In Chess Book of Chess Improvement
Lessons from the Best Players in the World's Leading Chess Magazine
Steve Giddins (editor) 336 pages - €22.95

The most didactic annotations by the world's best players of the past three decades, in thematic chapters.

"There is no doubt about it: the games and annotations really are top-notch and any player studying the material would definitely improve various aspects of their own play."
Sean Marsh, CHESS Magazine (UK)

Endgame Virtuoso Magnus Carlsen
His Extraordinary Skills Uncovered and Explained
Tibor Karolyi 272 pages - €24.95

"A real gem! Karolyi manages to entertain and instruct."
GM Karsten Muller, author of 'Fundamental Chess Endings'

"A fantastic book on Carlsen's endgame technique, from which one can learn a great deal." – *IM Dirk Schuh*

"Karolyi has a pleasant style of analysing: objective, not too many variations, with plenty of diagrams. He always ends with useful observations on Carlsen's play."
IM Hans Bohm, De Telegraaf, NL

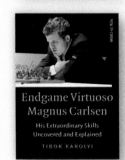

available at your local (chess)bookseller or at www.newinchess.com

OPENING ENCYCLOPAEDIA 2019

NEW LAYOUT, BETTER ACCESS, EXCITING VIDEOS

The Encyclopaedia can help you learn openings rapidly giving you a head start against your next opponents. Each article includes explanations and annotated games, which illustrate typical plans, to help deepen your understanding.

The concept of the opening article: A Grandmaster or International Master presents you a repertoire idea, shows all important variations and his analyses, explains typical plans and shows all the critical lines. Every article includes annotated model games selected by the author to illustrate the ideas in tournament practice.

The new Opening Encyclopaedia 2019 was completely revamped to enhance usability, with features such as a new design, new menu, and opening name sorting for fast and easy access to your favorite openings. Under the Menu "Ideas for your Repertoire" you can find all articles classified according to the opening names: "Open games", "Semi-open games", "Closed games", "Half -closed game", "Flank-Openings" or "English Opening and Reti". E.g. for the popular Najdorf Variation the Opening Encyclopaedia offers 41 opening articles. Each of it is accessible easily via "Semi-open games"- Siclian Defence – Najdorf Variation. As easy the user can switch from one article to the other to absorb all the important maneuvers and typical plans related to the variation. That way finding your favorite openings becomes easy and fast! Additionally, the new Encyclopaedia offers the traditional access to find openings from the "ECO-list" as an alternative access to all opening articles.

Also new: 20 high-class opening videos are included in the Encyclopaedia 2019, from our popular ChessBase Authors. You'll

find Daniel King, Simon Williams, Yannick Pelletier, Mihail Marin, Erwin l'Ami, presenting new opening ideas clear and vividly. The number of articles in the Opening Encyclopaedia is growing – it now contains more than 1,100 and the included games database contains all games from all the opening articles. This makes the new Opening Encyclopaedia 2019 an indispensable reference for every tournament player.

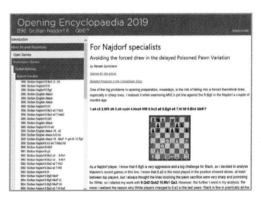

All innovations at a glance:

- Over 1,100 special theoretical databases
- 180 new opening surveys, a lot of them revised, in total 6,680 surveys
- Over 38,000 illustrative games
- Much improved usability: New design, new menu, new sorting of openings according to names for a fast and comfortable access
- 20 opening videos (total duration: 7 hours) of the most popular ChessBase Authors

Opening Encyclopaedia 2019 **99,90 €**

Update from
Opening Encyclopaedia 2018 **59,90 €**

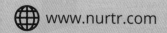

2019#5
NEW ♟ IN CHESS

5

'Most chess players tend to be good at chess only!'

8 GrandmasterChef
Thinking ahead and making plans while you're cooking, why not?

10 NIC'S Café
While Garry Kasparov is about to make his debut as a Manga star, Bobby Fischer remains an inspiration, too. This time for a young Icelandic chess musician.

12 Your Move
Bill Lombardy's advice to a young and promising player to study the endgame didn't fall on deaf ears.

14 Carlsen ruthless in Armageddon
In an undisguised attempt to fight draws and have more excitement, Altibox Norway Chess introduced a tiebreak system of Armageddon games. The Norwegian TV viewers loved the daily mayhem not in the last place because their hero Magnus Carlsen proved extremely efficient.

19 Celeb64: Peter Falk

30 Fair & Square
Courtney Love adores the horsey-shape piece that moves in an L shape.

42 Back to the Falklands
FIDE vice-president Nigel Short sincerely doubts whether Gens Una Sumus was high on their agenda when a group of Argentinian chess players secretly visited the Falklands.

46 Nepo wins first Grand Prix
With its walls draped in black and white, the Central Chess Club in Moscow was barely recognizable, but that did not stop the Russian participants to call the shots.

64 Secrets of Opening Surprises
Jeroen Bosch presents the improved Malinoise Defence.

68 Maximize Your Tactics
Find the right moves.

70 Shaking up the hierarchy
Alexandra Goryachkina turned the Women's Candidates Tournament into a one-horse race and earned the right to challenge World Champion Ju Wenjun.

76 Judit Polgar
What distinguishes Magnus Carlsen from his great predecessors?

80 When in Scotland...
The World Champion won a barrel of whisky at the Lindores Abbey Chess Stars.

88 The Blitz Whisperer
Maxim Dlugy examines what makes Maxime Vachier-Lagrave such a phenomenal speed chess player.

96 Chess Pattern Recognition
A far advanced rook pawn can be a considerable trump.

98 Sadler on Books
There are many ways to improve your play, but according to Matthew Sadler, studying the stars of our game remains a great recipe.

102 A tribute to Pal Benko
Jan Timman won first prize in the endgame study tournament that Pal Benko organized for his 90th birthday.

106 Just Checking
What was the best piece of advice Romain Edouard ever got?

CONTRIBUTORS TO THIS ISSUE
Simen Agdestein, Vishy Anand, Levon Aronian, Jeroen Bosch, Maxim Dlugy, Daniil Dubov, Romain Edouard, Anish Giri, Alexander Grischuk, John Henderson, Konstantin Landa, Ding Liren, Ian Nepomniachtchi, Peter Heine Nielsen, Maxim Notkin, Arthur van de Oudeweetering, Judit Polgar, Matthew Sadler, Nigel Short, Jan Timman, Yu Yangyi

GrandmasterChef

The BBC's culinary contest MasterChef started in 1990. The unlikely hit featuring top chefs competing against each other in the kitchen has gone on to become a big international phenomenon, exported to 60 different countries around the world. But who could have predicted that one day chess grandmasters would be judged by Michelin starred chefs!

The 'Chess Chefs' competition was organized for the second year running in conjunction with Altibox Norway Chess and the Foundation Chef of the Year Norway, with an edited version filmed for Norwegian broadcaster TV 2. Each team of two grandmasters was paired up with one of the country's top chefs — each a candidate to represent Norway at the Bocuse d'Or, the celebrated World Championship of cooking — to produce a creative dish with salmon.

Although this was a fun event on the rest-day, the competition was fierce, with the concentration level just as intense over the chopping board for the players than it is over the chessboard, as can be seen in the eyes of Magnus Carlsen and Alexander Grischuk, who were paired with Chef Christian André Pettersen, a previous Bocuse d'Or medallist.

The Grandmaster Chef is unquestionably Vishy Anand, who for the second year running won the culinary contest, only this year joined by Maxime Vachier-Lagrave (and Chef Filip August Bendi), as they served up a winning Salmon à la Chennai. ∎

Manga chess star

The internationally renowned Cannes Film Festival had an added attraction this year, with the arrival on the red carpet of none other than Garry Kasparov. The former World Champion was there to help launch a new venture where he will star as one of new heroes of *Blitz*, a chess-themed manga series that's about to be released into the Japanese anime world.

Manga chess is easier when Garry Kasparov is watching your back.

It was all the brainchild of Nice film producer Cédric Biscay. A sport, youth and love affairs constitute a proven manga recipe for success, and the Frenchman decided that his graphic novels would be centred around the chess world – and who better a figure to be the guiding, inspirational character for the series than Garry Kasparov?

Not only did Kasparov agree to appear in the graphic novels, he's also voicing his own character in the anime film, and will also act as the technical advisor for all the chess scenes. 'I'm still dedicated to democratizing chess, and this is a unique opportunity to do so, especially in Japan, where it is not really popular and where Shogi is better known',

says Kasparov. Five of the fifteen volumes are already completed, and the first manga graphic novel is due to be released by February 2020, with the anime film expected by 2021.

Blitz will follow the life of Tom, a young college student looking to get closer to chess fan Harmony, who shows no interest in him. So he will do everything he can to learn chess in the hope of getting closer to her. And this is where Garry Kasparov comes into the action – when viewing the chess legend through virtual reality glasses, an unexpected event transfers all of his chess knowledge and skills into young Tom's mind.

Jazz, nice!

A touch of melodic, soothing jazz is always nice – and all the nicer when you discover that Bobby Fischer's life story proved to be the inspiration behind the debut album from Mikael Máni, a new fresh-faced Icelandic jazz guitarist.

Máni graduated from the Conservatory in Amsterdam last summer under the tutelage of Dutch jazz guitarist legend Jesse van Ruller. He's tipped as one to watch, and along with his older Icelandic cats Skúli Sverisson (bass) and Magnús Trygvason Eliassen (drums and vibraphone), he formed The Mikael Máni Trio.

Mikael Máni in Bobby Fischer's corner in Reykjavik's Bókin bookshop.

Their first album, filled with Máni's own compositions, is called 'Bobby' and its release at the end of May was celebrated with a concert at the Reykjavik Harpa Concert Hall, also the venue for the Reykjavik International Open.

The album comes with a cover picture taken outside of the Reykjavik bookshop Bókin, where Fischer was a regular customer and which still has his favourite chair, where the 11th World Champion would be left alone with his thoughts. The track list of 'Bobby' includes titles such as *Board Games, Reykjavik 1972* and others that freely hint at the inspiration of the album.

The Reykjavik Grapevine described 'Bobby' as having '[...] atmospheric, melodic richness that suggests it could also sit comfortably in the record collections of Tortoise, Nick Drake or Lambchop fans.'

Can't take it with you

There's many who like to open their newspapers just to read an obituary of a well-lived life – and similarly, we were taken by *The New York Times* obituary of Lewis B. Cullman, the investment banker and arts patron extraordinaire, who died in early June at the ripe old age of 100, but not before giving millions to cultural and educational institutes in New York City over many years and helped charities raise millions more for worthy causes.

Born into wealth, Lewis B. Cullman was the scion of the family that owned the Benson & Hedges and Philip Morris tobacco companies – but he was determined to make his own fortune on Wall Street, and did so in the 1960s by heading a company that produced and sold desk calendars and appointment books, and through this success he went on to sit on the boards of the Metropolitan Museum of Art, the Museum of Modern Art, the New York Botanical Garden and many hospitals, universities and corporations.

Lewis B. Cullman donated an
estimated $28 million to chess.

By his own admission, the favourite of
all the charities he was involved with
was the Chess in the Schools initiative.
Founded in 1986 by Fan Adams Jr., a
Mobil Oil executive, and legendary
chess coach Bruce Pandolfini, the
trailblazing program took chess into
the classroom, reaching tens of thousands of students.

In his 2004 memoir, *Can't Take
It With You: The Art of Making and
Giving Money*, Cullman explains why
he had contributed an estimated $28
million over the years to it: 'Chess
develops critical thinking. It was the
concept of using chess as an educational tool that appealed to me.'

Fake news

Speaking of *The New York
Times* obituary pages, another
caught our attention: Sylvia
Miles, the flamboyant, noir-
faced Hollywood actress who died on
9 June aged 94. Everything was there
in the obit for the two-time Academy
Award nominee (for *Midnight Cowboy*
and *Farewell, My Lovely*), including
her garish dress-sense, bawdy nature,
her life as an Andy Warhol groupie,
excessive party-goer... and even her
prowess over the chessboard!

According to the *NYT*, 'Ms. Miles
was a competitive chess player, partic-
ipating in tournaments and earning
a mention in a 1972 feature article on
female players in *The Times* and in the
newspaper's chess column in 1968.'
This left some in the US chess scene

scratching their head in bemuse-
ment. And they had every right to be
bemused, because the newspaper was
caught out by its own fake news!

One of Miles' many talents was that
she was a notorious self-publicist. She
made up many stories to get into the
media in the early 1970s, at a time
when it was much harder to double-
check facts accurately.

A little prudent fact-checking for
her obit would have revealed that the
actress was called out on her chess
prowess by Rex Reed, in his 1974
book, *People Are Crazy Here*. In it, the
celebrity profiler describes how Miles
would do anything to see her name
in the media: 'She told everyone she
played chess with Bobby Fischer,

The inimitable Sylvia Miles.
Chess, how difficult can it be?

probably as good as Bobby Fischer
even, and by golly, a few days later
there she was, listed in *The New York
Times* as one of the ten top female
chess players in America.'

Rediscovered

The Lewis Chessmen are
considered to be among the
finest group of medieval
chess pieces ever recov-
ered from the antiquities. They were
found in 1831 on a beach on the north
side of the Isle of Lewis in the Outer
Hebrides. Valued as 'priceless', they
are now on display in the British
Museum in London, and the National
Museum of Scotland in Edinburgh.

A total of 93 objects were in the
original hoard before they ended

up where they rightly belong, in
museums. But en route to getting
there, they did have various adventures in the 19th century, and five
pieces were known to be missing.
And now like an amazing find on
BBC's *Antiques Roadshow*, one has
miraculously resurfaced again after a
gap of 200 years, after it was unknow-
ingly kept hidden in a drawer by an
Edinburgh family.

After authenticating the missing
piece as genuine, Sotheby's put the
piece up for auction, and in early
July, it was sold to an anonymous
telephone bidder for £735,000. The
missing piece, measuring 8.8 cm in
height, is a Lewis warder and was
purchased for £5, about £100 in
today's money.

The family, who also wish to remain
anonymous, had no idea the object was
one of the long-lost Lewis Chessmen.
The piece, made from walrus tusk,
was bought by the family's grandfa-
ther, an antiques dealer, in 1964. He
similarly had no idea of its signifi-
cance, and he passed it down to his
family. They have looked after it for
55 years without realizing its importance, before taking it to Sotheby's
auction house in London during one
of their free valuation days.

Sotheby's expert Alexander Kader,
who examined the piece, said his 'jaw

'Oh, my goodness, it's one
of the Lewis Chessmen.'

dropped' when he realized what they
had in their possession. 'I said, "Oh
my goodness, it's one of the Lewis
Chessmen".' ∎

Bill and Bobby

As I was reading professor Joseph Ponterotto's touching article about Bobby Fischer and William Lombardy in New In Chess 2019/3, I recalled my meeting with the latter during the 2016 World Championship match in New York.

During the fourth match game, we heard a man arguing quite loudly with a woman who was reluctant to let him into the hall. The man claimed that he had been the second of Bobby Fischer. Coming closer and seeing him I confirmed to the official that this was the famous grandmaster William Lombardy. Admittedly, he was in quite bad shape after having been evicted from his apartment some time ago, which he also mentioned. A few minutes later another kind female official wanted to take him to a shop to dress him up with some new clothes, which I hope actually happened.

Meanwhile Lombardy was eager to talk about the past. Standing with the great view of the spectators' area towards Brooklyn Bridge, he confirmed to me that Bobby had somehow come that way, across that bridge, when Lombardy first met him in the Manhattan Chess Club. The youngster, 11 or 12 years of age, had immediately told him that he wanted

to become World Champion of chess.

'Then first of all, you have to study the endgame, I told him. And when I was back to the club next week, Bobby had piled up all the endgame books of the club library. Then I realized that he was serious about this', Lombardy explained to me.

I could not find any reference to this very early meeting in my sources on Fischer or Lombardy, so I am not sure this story is known. If it is not, I think it should be.

Øystein Brekke
Åmot, Norway

Two things to ponder

I am not sure what went wrong with your research for NIC's Café in issue 2019/4, but many of your readers (especially in the United Kingdom and Southeast Asia) will be aware that Siam/Thailand never was a British colonial state. Indeed, Thailand is famously the only Southeast Asian country never to have been colonised by any Western power.

The report on Extinction Rebellion is also intriguing. Single use plastic is one big problem. Is there anything that can be done about the plastic wrapper the magazine arrives in? I also wonder how much thought chess authorities are giving to the question

of human induced climate change. It is generally considered that one thing the individual can do to help is to give up flying. This would obviously have a devastating effect on international chess as currently constituted. Something to ponder.

Aidan Woodger
Halifax, United Kingdom

Chess erudition

In New In Chess 2019/4, page 103, Jan Timman rightly notes that Magnus Carlsen is impressively erudite chesswise, and that it is a part of his success. He remarks that in the game Keymer-Carlsen, Grenke Classic 2019, the swap on c3 (13...♗xc3) cannot be considered as a surprise, as Carlsen had read the book *Timman's Titans*, with comments on this move which has already occurred in at least three other games: Bronstein-Petrosian (Amsterdam 1956), Donner-Petrosian (Santa Monica 1966) and Timman-Tal (Tallinn 1973).

One could add that this manoeuvre has also been presented in another excellent book, *Techniques of Positional Play: 45 Practical Methods to Gain the Upper Hand in Chess* (Bronznik and Terekhin, New In Chess 2013), p. 28-31, where it is described as 'Technique no. 4 – The

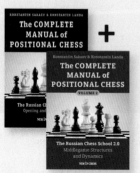

bishop cage after ...♗g7xc3! b2xc3', including two other examples: Shamis-Pelts (Kharkov 1967) and Forintos-Gligoric (Ljubljana 1969).

Michel de Saboulin
Sceaux, France

Disarm Armageddon

Baker Blitz is a superior solution for chess tiebreaks. This new variation of chess will solve two of chess's biggest problems:

1) Too many classical draws.

2) Armageddon (which many top players recognize as a coin flip and not earned victory, since Black has a decisive advantage. And is it fun to root for your favourite player to draw?)

Baker Chess consists of two-game matches with one amount of time. So, in Baker Blitz:

– Each player begins with 10 minutes on the clock, during which two games must be played (White & Black).

– The amount of time a player uses in the first game determines the amount left for the second game (when colours are switched). (E.g. if one player uses 7 minutes, he has 3 minutes for the next game.)

One way of looking at chess is that the player who presents the most problems usually wins. In the past there was no reward for having this initiative. Baker chess rewards the player who takes the initiative with more time for the second game.

Try Baker Chess. Play a few matches with a friend, and you will quickly see how it can be an improvement over Armageddon chess. Baker Chess is fun! Do you know of anyone who plays Armageddon chess for fun?

Billy Woodward
Lexington, KY, USA

Show, don't tell

Regarding the game from Round 1 in the TePe Sigeman tournament in Malmö between GM Nihal Sarin and GM Ivan Saric – as described in New In Chess 2019/4 – I think the editors were asleep – a fairly unusual experi-ence from my decades of reading your magazine! I will concede that GM Nils Grandelius might have forgotten more about chess than NotMaster Rea knows about this wonderful game, but does this excuse the

Write to us
New In Chess, P.O. Box 1093
1810 KB Alkmaar, The Netherlands
or e-mail: editors@newinchess.com
Letters may be edited or abridged

appending '??' to 67.♕a6+ without demonstrating the obviously winning alternative?

Nihal Sarin
Ivan Saric
Malmö 2019 (1)

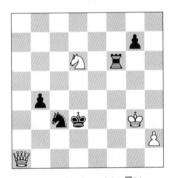

position after 66...♖f6

I am confident that White is aware that the move he played turned out to be costly – and yet, to win the game, he needs to win the g-pawn, the knight, or the rook, without allowing the advanced b-pawn to do any damage. Obviously, queens are better than rooks, but there do seem to be extenuating circumstances in this position that make the win not exactly simple?!

It seems likely that if the obvious 67.♘e8 is so great, White might well have played that, but it is not all roses for White after 67.♘e8 ♖e6. Addi-tionally, Black can play to allow the trade of knights and loss of his b-pawn, provided the black king can make it back to f7. After which Black

has a known fortress shuffling rook from h6/f6 while keeping the g-pawn on g7 and using the king to patrol g8. I am not ready to make the claim that the position after 66...♖f6 is a draw, Black has much to prove as well!! But dumping 67.♕a6+ under the bus without presenting a winning alter-native is below your usual standard.

I very much appreciate the continued tradition of excellence at NIC, thanks!

Andrew Rea
Alexandria, VA, USA

Editorial postscript:

Point taken. The position after 67.♘e8 ♖e6 68.♘c7 should be winning for White. After 68...♖f6 69.♕a5 b3 70.♘d5 ♘xd5 71.♕xd5+ the exchange of knights would lead to a draw if the black king were close to his g7-pawn (as pointed out by Mr. Rea), but as it is not Black is lost: 71...♔c3 72.♕c5+ ♔b2 73.♕d4+ ♔a2 74.♕a4+ ♔b2 75.h4 ♖g6+ 76.♔f4 ♖f6+ 77.♔g5 and the g-pawn will soon fall, breaking Black's fortress. ■

COLOPHON

PUBLISHER: Allard Hoogland
EDITOR-IN-CHIEF:
Dirk Jan ten Geuzendam
HONORARY EDITOR: Jan Timman
CONTRIBUTING EDITOR: Anish Giri
EDITORS: Peter Boel, René Olthof
PRODUCTION: Joop de Groot
TRANSLATORS: Ken Neat, Piet Verhagen
SALES AND ADVERTISING: Remmelt Otten

PHOTOS AND ILLUSTRATIONS IN THIS ISSUE:
Josef Arnost, Maria Emelianova, Tristan Fewings/Sotheby's, Eteri Kublashvili, Lennart Ootes, Niki Riga, Berend Vonk

COVER PHOTO: Niki Riga

© No part of this magazine may be reproduced, stored in a retrieval system or transmitted in any form or by any means, recording or otherwise, without the prior permission of the publisher.

NEW IN CHESS
P.O. BOX 1093
1810 KB ALKMAAR
THE NETHERLANDS

PHONE: 00-31-(0)72-51 27 137
SUBSCRIPTIONS: nic@newinchess.com
EDITORS: editors@newinchess.com
ADVERTISING: otten@newinchess.com

WWW.NEWINCHESS.COM

LENNART OOTES

In an undisguised attempt to fight draws and have more excitement, Altibox Norway Chess introduced a tiebreak system of Armageddon games. The number of draws was not reduced (on the contrary), but the viewers of Norway's TV2 loved the daily mayhem. Not in the last place because their Magnus Carlsen proved extremely efficient in the Armageddons and took first prize. **SIMEN AGDESTEIN** reports from Stavanger.

World Champion wins Norway Chess as he excels in experimental tiebreak system

Carlsen ruthless in Armageddon

In an improvised speech at the closing dinner, Magnus Carlsen said that he liked the new format because it had suited him very well.

The aim of Altibox Norway Chess, right from its inception in 2013, has always been to stage the strongest 10-player tournament in the world. To achieve this aim, the organizers in Stavanger try to invite the 10 highest-rated players in the January world rankings. They have always been very successful in their ambitions, and this year, too, they managed to have almost all the players they coveted. Only Anish Giri had to decline the invitation due to his busy schedule, and Vladimir Kramnik was not available, because that January he had announced his retirement from chess.

Because it is hard to top a tournament with the best players, Norway Chess mainly competes with its own previous editions. The conditions couldn't get very much better either, with the beautiful fjords and scenic surroundings in Stavanger on the west coast of Norway. The players get their own cool car with the flashy Norway Chess design, plus a driver, there was a boat trip and a cooking competition on the free day and the pay is great. Everything is set for historic battles.

Alas, experience has shown that this is not always enough. The top players surely are artists, but they rarely lose. When you bring together only the best, the results aren't necessarily great entertainment. I am talking about the high number of draws, of course.

In Norway, chess has become a big TV-hit. Norwegians love to see Norwegians win, no matter the sport or whether they understand what's going on. Almost a million viewers followed the peak moments of the World Championship matches with Magnus Carlsen. But there is a limit to their enthusiasm, and eventually people will not find it fascinating to watch long draws.

Therefore, Norway Chess had come up with an innovative format, an experiment to create more excite-

ment. To begin with, the games had a new time limit: two hours per player for the entire game and only from move 40 onwards a 10-second increment per move. This mostly meant no time for going to the toilet or anything except for rapidly making moves once move 40 was reached.

A win in these classical games brought two points. In case of a draw

The players generally reacted favourably to the format. Magnus Carlsen liked it because it worked so well for him, but others also saw opportunities. As Alexander Grischuk put it, 'It is fine. The only thing is that it killed the intrigue, because Magnus is just unstoppable with this format. But that's not a complaint, that's just an observation.

Alexander Grischuk: 'It is fine. The only thing is that it killed the intrigue, because Magnus is just unstoppable with this format.'

the players got 20 minutes to catch their breath and then had to play an Armageddon tiebreaker, with White having 10 minutes against Black's seven and Black having draw odds. And no increments till move 60, after which two seconds per move were added. The winner of the Armageddon game got 1½ points, the loser ½ point.

Regarding the score, I would prefer 3-2-1-0, as they have in the NHL.'

And Maxime Vachier-Lagrave opined: 'It's good to have a tiebreaker, but if you want fewer draws, you might make it less favourable to win in the Armageddon, to push victories in the classical games. I wouldn't mind if a couple of events had

First he was annoyed by the way he had played in the decisive game of the blitz tournament, then Magnus Carlsen stood up straight and congratulated Maxime Vachier-Lagrave on his victory.

tiebreaks after the games, as long as you emphasize the classical games. And the time-control in the classical games here made some of us play faster and therefore more safely, which in fact leads to more draws.'

But some players were less enthusiastic. Said Wesley So: 'In classical chess with top players it's unavoidable to have 80 per cent draws, so I guess people complain about the draws. I was not really comfortable with the format, because switching from classical chess to blitz chess right away is quite difficult for me, particularly with these players, who play a lot of blitz.'

Ding Liren also had his reservations: 'This concept affects the quality of the classical games. Not because we are already thinking about the Armageddon games when we are playing the classical games, but because our judgement and calculations diminish when we play these games on the same day. I would prefer just classical games or have Armageddon games as a tiebreaker at the end of the tournament for players who have scored the same number of points.'

In fact, the organizers had already listened to the players for this first experiment. Originally, the Armageddon games were going to be played at the end of the round, but at the suggestion of Grischuk ('I am not only a player, but I also like watching chess') it was decided in a unanimous vote at the players' meeting that the Armageddon games would be played shortly after a classical game had ended in a draw.

Blitz ace MVL

But let's begin with the beginning. As is custom in Stavanger, the drawing of lots was a blitz tournament on the eve of the first round. As is commonly known, Magnus Carlsen wants to be the number one in everything, even when playing soccer or tennis, but in blitz he faces fierce competition from Maxime Vachier-Lagrave, who beat him twice in the Abidjan leg of the

In the 33 Armageddon games White won 15 and Black prevailed either by drawing (13) or winning (6) in 19 games.

Grand Chess Tour and in Stavanger even overtook him in the world blitz rankings, which he now tops with a phenomenal 2948 rating.

Before the last round MVL was leading his arch-rival by half a point, and needed a draw to secure first place. Obviously, Magnus went for sharp play and eventually he got his chance.

Magnus Carlsen
Maxime Vachier-Lagrave
Stavanger Blitz 2019 (9)

position after 27...♖e8

28.f5? I followed the game on *chess24* with comments by Peter Svidler and Jan Gustafsson and it

Stavanger 2019 blitz

1 Maxime Vachier-Lagrave	2921	7½	3057
2 Levon Aronian	2827	6	2912
3 Magnus Carlsen	2923	6	2899
4 Shakhriyar Mamedyarov	2757	5	2828
5 Ding Liren	2773	4½	2781
6 Yu Yangyi	2705	3½	2709
7 Wesley So	2759	3½	2707
8 Fabiano Caruana	2804	3	2655
9 Vishy Anand	2747	3	2661
10 Alexander Grischuk	2750	3	2660

didn't take long for the eight-time Russian Champion to spot that all the tricks were in White's favour after 28.♘d7!. They work even after 28... e3 29.♕xe3. **28...♕xc5! 29.♕c7 ♕f8! 30.♕xc6**

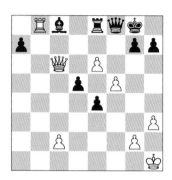

30...♗d7! This clears it up. **31.♕xd7 ♖xb8 32.e7** Magnus never gives up too early, but he's a whole rook behind. **32...♕e8 33.♕xd5+ ♔h8 34.♕e5 ♖b6 35.♕xe4 ♖f6** 0-1.

Magnus stood up, shook his head in disbelief at his overly risky play and then congratulated MVL on his win. MVL won the blitz tournament with 7½ points, ahead of Aronian and Carlsen on 6 points, and interestingly chose starting number 4 to have White in his game against Carlsen.

There was some discussion about whether it was better to be Black or White in the Armageddons, which then led to the question which starting number was the best, since the Armageddon games would be played with the same colour as the classical game. Magnus preferred Black, while MVL and Caruana thought White was advantageous. Levon Aronian initially also preferred White, but after the tournament he wasn't so sure. The statistics of the classical games highlighted the impression from the Carlsen-Caruana match that 'Black is the new White', as Black seemed to be pushing in most games. In the 33 Armageddon games White won 15 and Black prevailed either by drawing (13) or winning (6) in 19 games.

Hopelessly tired

For Magnus, the new Armageddon format worked very well; it seemed to fit him like a glove. It didn't matter which colour he was. He could calmly accept that most of his classical games ended in a draw, since he was confident he would win in the Armageddon. It may have helped that people again and again tried to beat his new favourite weapon, the Sveshnikov Variation in the Sicilian.

In the 'confession booth', the Norwegian TV's invention where the players can tell their thoughts during the game, Carlsen said that he is hopelessly tired of this opening, but as long as it serves him well, he might just as well continue to play it. Actually, in the classical game against Aronian he was apparently dead lost, but Aronian got into time-trouble and Magnus managed to save the draw. In the Armageddon just after that, Magnus was back on top again.

NOTES BY
Peter Heine Nielsen

Levon Aronian
Magnus Carlsen
Stavanger 2019 (2, Armageddon)
Sicilian Defence, Rossolimo Attack

Forcing a result in an Armageddon game if the classical game had ended in a draw was an interesting experiment that posed lots of challenges to the players. Less than 30 minutes after an often, as in this example, gruelling classical game with emotional ups and downs, the players had to readjust and get ready for completely new circumstances. The slow pace of the previous game is changed to a much faster format, the scoring of the game has changed in the sense that only two results are possible: White winning the game or Black taking the full point with either a draw or a win. On top of that,

the colours were not reversed, which meant that there often was a repetition of the opening duel in the first game, with the players either armed with a few pointers from their on-site or online seconds, or having rushed to their rooms for a lightning check on their engines. Considering that the players also have basic human needs, such as getting something to eat in the brief break between games, one can only be impressed with the general level of play despite the focus on the Armageddon blunders – especially in this game.

1.e4!?
Aronian has been known as a 1.d4/c4/♘f3 player, but has recently managed to add 1.e4 to his repertoire.
1...c5 2.♘f3 ♘c6 3.♗b5
Caruana's choice in his first three White games in the World Championship match. Because Black did well there, the pendulum swung to 3.d4, but now, in Norway Chess, both Aronian and, later, Caruana managed to create opening problems for Magnus.
3...g6 4.♗xc6 dxc6 5.d3

5...♗g7!?
By far the main move, but in the classical game Magnus had experimented with the much rarer 5...♕c7!? 6.0-0 e5. The point of omitting 5...♗g7 is precisely that Black's bishop keeps a choice, and, as in the game, gives Black the flexibility of using it on the f8-a3 diagonal. But Aronian manages to put his finger on a sore spot: 7.♗e3 ♘f6 8.♕e1 ♗g4 9.♘bd2 ♘h5 10.a3 ♗e7. Around here, Magnus went to

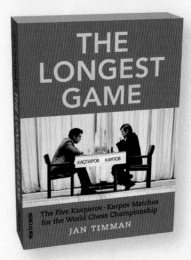

the confession booth, saying that he quite liked his position, because it wasn't really clear what White should do next? 11.♕b1!

ANALYSIS DIAGRAM

This move convincingly answered that question. The problem with the bishop not being on g7 is highlighted after 11...a5 12.b4!, when after 12...axb4 13.axb4 ♖xa1, 14.♕xa1 attacks the e5-pawn, and, even worse, after 12...cxb4 13.axb4 ♗xb4? 14.♕xb4! axb4 15.♖xa8+ also wins the rook on h8, again due to the bishop missing on g7.

6.h3 e5 7.0-0 ♕c7!?

Different timing, but the same idea. Black wants to protect the e5-pawn, giving himself the option of putting the knight on f6. Aronian had to battle it twice, but seemed to like it so much that he actually tried it out with colours reversed against Caruana!

8.♗e3

With two hours for the game unlike Aronian's 10 minutes, Caruana came up with 8.a3!? against Magnus in Round 9. This seems harmless enough, but after 8...♘f6 9.♗e3 c4 10.♘c3 cxd3 11.♕xd3 0-0 12.♖fd1 ♖e8 13.♗c5 ♗f8 14.♗xf8 ♔xf8

15.♖d2 Caruana did create some opening problems for Magnus.

8...b6 9.♘bd2 ♘e7!

This may seem illogical, but since White has set himself up for attacking the e5-pawn with ♘c4 after ...♘f6, Magnus switches plans and aims for an attack with ...f5, because White's misplaced bishop on e3 will gain him some time based on the ...f4 threat.

10.a3 0-0 11.b4 cxb4 12.axb4 f5 13.♘c4 ♗e6 14.♘g5 ♗d7

15.♕e2?!

My main point is that this game generally has the quality of a classical game, but this move might still illustrate a difference. It looks logical, but it serves no specific purpose and plays into Black's hands. Given more time, Aronian would probably have played 15.♖a3!?, after which ♕a1 exerts pressure both on e5 and along the a-file. And if 15...h6 16.♘f3 f4 17.♗d2 g5 18.♗c3 ♘g6 then 19.d4 has a lot more force than in the game.

15...h6 16.♘f3 f4 17.♗d2 g5 18.♗c3 ♘g6 19.d4

The passive 19.♘h2 was to be considered, but Aronian logically plays in

MAGNUS CARLSEN FELT VERY MUCH AT HOME IN THE NEW FORMAT

the centre to counter Black's attack on the flank.

19...exd4 20.♗xd4

20...g4!

In an ideal world, Black would like ...h5 and ...g4, but in a sharp battle where every tempo counts, one cannot care about trifles like pawn structure, so the World Champion hurries to create some threats.

21.hxg4 ♗xg4 22.c3?!

As on move 15, a logical move to cover the d4-bishop. However, 22.♘cd2!, while looking like a retreat, protects its colleague on f3, and meets 22...♗xd4 with 23.♕c4+!.

22...c5 23.bxc5 bxc5 24.♗xg7 ♕xg7 25.♘d6

The point of White's play is that 25...♘h4? is now met by 26.♕c4+, but Magnus played:

25...♔h8!

26.♘f5!?

This pawn sacrifice seems to deflect Black's attention from the kingside just in time, because after 26...♗xf5 27.exf5 ♖xf5 Black's threats have disappeared and, for example. 28.♕d3 gives full compensation.

26...♖xf5!

This, however, is a rude awakening. Black now has the bishop on g4 instead of the rook on f8, which means imminent threats to the white king, with ...♗xf3 as the obvious but hard-to-handle threat.

27.exf5 ♘h4

28.f6!

Objectively the best move, but 28.♖xa7!? deserves to be mentioned, because 28...♗xf3! 29.♖xa8+ ♔h7, although it looks crushing, actually allows the amusing 30.♖a7!, when White very much stays in the game, even though Black is better after 30...♕xa7 31.♕d3!? (31.gxf3? ♕g7+ mates).

28...♕xf6

29.♖a6?!

Black again threatened ...♗xf3, followed by a mating attack on the g-file, and Aronian tries to maximize his counterplay as quickly as possible. Objectively better, however, was 29.♖fe1! ♗xf3 30.♖a6!!, since after 30...♕g7 or 30...♕g5, 31.♕e5!+ keeps White very much in the game. Easiest is 30...♖xe2 31.♖xf6 ♔g7 32.♖xf4 ♘g6 33.♖f5 ♗d3 34.♖xc5 a5, when stopping Black's passed pawn will

Celeb 64

John Henderson

Peter Falk

'Just one more thing...' That was the famous catchphrase from the self-deprecating, dishevelled detective Lt. Columbo, so memorably portrayed by Peter Falk. Everyone's favourite TV detective was also a big favourite in my own household when I was a kid – especially being new to chess in the aftermath of the Fischer-Spassky match, and one of the early *Columbo* classics having a chess theme. In 'The Most Dangerous Match' from 1973 the near-lifeless body of a jovial Russian grandmaster is found in the back alley of an international hotel just as he is scheduled to play a match against his flighty American rival. Amidst some wonderful chess scenes, Columbo cracked the case, and that was no coincidence, for Falk was a chess aficionado at heart. He took lessons in the early 70s from a National Master and was a spectator at two big California events: the American Open in Santa Monica in 1972 and the US Open in Pasadena in 1983 – at the latter he was photographed deep in conversation with Viktor Kortchnoi. The multi-Emmy winning actor was also photographed kibitzing with Yasser Seirawan at the same event, as can be seen on the cover of the December 1983 *Chess Life*. Falk also owned the film rights to the Fischer-Spassky match and tasked Oscar-winning director Milos Forman to do the movie, plans which unfortunately had to be abandoned due to technical issues. ∎

take so much effort that White has no realistic hopes of winning. Which begs the question of whether it is even relevant to discuss lines in which White saves a draw in an Armageddon game?

29...♕g7 30.♖xh6+ ♕xh6 31.♕e5+ ♕g7

32.♕xg7+?! Much better was 32.♘xh4!, because, unlike in the game, White's knight will not get into trouble after 32...♕xe5 33.♘g6+ ♔g7 34.♘xe5. Yet Black will easily get the desired draw anyway.

32...♔xg7 33.♘xh4 a5! 34.♖a1 a4 35.♖a3 ♔f6

36.♔f1

The computer says that White's best chance by far is 36.♘f3, but that's a chance to make a worthless draw,

The day after the last round the players visited a massive school chess competition. Guess who had to pose for most selfies and sign most autographs?

since after 36...♗xf3 37.gxf3 White's winning chances are obviously zero. Aronian does what he has to do, but so does Magnus:

36...♔e5 37.♔e1 ♔d5 38.f3 ♗h5 39.♔d2 ♗e8 40.♔c1 ♔c4 41.♘f5 ♖a6 42.♘g7 ♗g6 43.♔d2 ♔d5

The confusion he tried to create only got his knight trapped, and White resigned.

The question is to what standard we should judge such games? During their nationwide broadcast, Norwegian TV2 had no doubt that they made for great television.

■ ■ ■

Magnus secured tournament victory with one round to go by beating his closest contender Yu Yangyi in the penultimate round. Perhaps Magnus eased off a bit in the last round, when his non-losing streak was very close to being destroyed. In classical games, his last loss was against Mamedyarov in Biel in 2018, and he has now gone 69 games on the trot.

Fabiano Caruana
Magnus Carlsen
Stavanger 2019 (9)

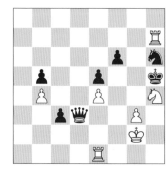

position after 49...c3

As Magnus pointed out after the game, Caruana could have mated

Is it even relevant to discuss lines in which White saves a draw in an Armageddon game?

him with 50.♘f5 ♛d2+ 51.♔f3! ♛xe1 52.g4+ ♔g5 53.♖g7 mate. 51...♛d3+ 52.♔f2 ♛d2+ 53.♖e2 would also have led to a mating attack, e.g. 53...♛d3 54.♖xh6+ ♔g4 55.♖h4+ ♔g5 56.♖h7, followed by 57.♖g7+ and 58.g4, mate. **50.♘f3 ♛c2+ 51.♔h3**

51...♔g6 Now it's Magnus's turn to miss a golden opportunity. The computer points out 51...♛b3! as winning for Black. Peter Svidler opined this was 'an absolutely futuristic idea' and that it wasn't 'humanly possible' to find such a move. **52.♖c7 ♘f7 53.♘h4+ ♔g7 54.♘f5+ ♔g6 55.♘h4+ ♔g7 56.♘f5+** ½-½.

In the Armageddon game, Caruana got his revenge by beating Magnus, sweet comfort for the American and an annoying end of the tournament for Magnus.

Obviously, the Armageddon games were a huge factor. But were there fewer draws than normal in the classical games? The 45 classical games saw seven White and four Black wins, a percentage of 76, which is actually the highest ever in the history of Norway Chess.

Whether we got more entertainment is a subjective question, but the Armageddons were certainly thrilling. Personally, I enjoyed seeing the world's best players making horrible mistakes. It's good to see that even the very best can lose their head.

For the final scores with the Armageddons, please see the cross-table at the end of this article. With the classical games only, the following final standings would have been reached:

1-2: Carlsen, Ding Liren: 5½ (+2);
3-4: Caruana, So: 5 (+1);
5-6: Aronian, Yu Yangyi: 4½ (50%);
7-8: MVL, Anand: 4 (-1)
9-10: Mamedyarov, Grischuk: 3½ (-2)

Magnus's win in the new format, three points ahead of Aronian and Yu, seems convincing, but with the old format Magnus would have shared the win with Ding Liren, with Caruana and So just half a point behind. Magnus won only two classical games and actually lost a few rating points. His best performance was probably the following:

NOTES BY
Peter Heine Nielsen

Magnus Carlsen
Alexander Grischuk
Stavanger 2019 (3)
Grünfeld-Indian Defence, Exchange Variation

1.d4 ♘f6 2.c4 g6 3.♘c3 d5!

A curious moment. For the past few years, Norway Chess has used a 'confession booth', intended for the players to give messages to the spectators during the games. Magnus

took it a step further: 'This is a small shout-out to Peter Heine, who thought Grischuk would play the King's Indian, and not the Grünfeld: Clown!' The Norwegian media, always on the look-out for stories, took it seriously and, as journalistic fairness dictates, contacted me during the game asking for a rebuttal! **4.cxd5 ♘xd5 5.e4 ♘xc3 6.bxc3 ♗g7 7.♗e3 c5 8.♖c1**

8...♛a5 Grischuk stays loyal to his preferred move, but in the next round Mamedyarov tried 8...0-0 against Magnus, both in the classical and the Armageddon game: 9.♘f3 ♘d7 10.♗e2 ♛a5 11.0-0 ♛xa2 12.♘d2 ♛a5 13.h4!? b5 14.h5 ♗b7 15.h6!

ANALYSIS DIAGRAM

was the classical game. I recently attributed the modern appreciation

Magnus took it a step further: 'This is a small shout-out to Peter Heine, who thought Grischuk would play the King's indian, and not the Grünfeld: Clown!'

of flank pawn attacks to AlphaZero, and some people pointed out to me that opening the h-file and giving mate is not exactly a new concept in chess! A fair point, so this diagram is a good opportunity to point out what AlphaZero has a preference for, according to Sadler and Regan in their book *Game Changer*. Precisely! Not going for a direct assault on the h-file but instead slowly and more cunningly putting the pawn on h6, effectively closing the h-file and instead aiming for a slower and more long-term attack. The benefits are numerous: it controls space in the critical area next to Black's king, cramping his defence, and, as in this game, forcing the bishop to h8, where it blocks the king's potential retreat. Moreover, in tactical sequences the pawn is only two squares away from queening. Not at all as direct as the typical hxg6 and mate along the h-file, but sometimes much more

powerful. And this game is a good illustration: 15...♗h8 16.e5 ♕c7 17.♗xb5! ♗xg2 18.♔xg2 ♕b7+ 19.♕f3 ♕xb5 20.♖b1 ♕a6 21.♘e4 cxd4 22.cxd4 f6 23.♘g5!.

ANALYSIS DIAGRAM

The 'cramped' nature of Black's kingside is making itself felt with 24. ♕d5+ being a deadly threat. And after 23...fxg5 24.♕d5+ e6 25.♕xd7 Black's position would be hopeless, with the bishop on h8 practically dead due to the pawns on d4, e5 and h6.

Mamedyarov successfully confused the issue with 23...e6, upon which Magnus blundered with 24.♖a1?, having missed 24...b6!. Instead, 24.♕b7! would have been deadly, because after the queen swap with 24...♕xb7+ 25.♖xb7 ♘xe5 there is the strong 26.♘xe6!. And if 24...♕e2, then 25.♕xd7 wins, since there is no perpetual after 25...♕g4+ 26.♔h2 fxg5 27.f3!: if Black takes twice on f3, White forces an easy endgame with 29.♕xe6+, again because the bishop is locked in on h8.
9.♕d2 0-0 10.♘f3 ♗g4!?

Grischuk's pet line, which he used twice in Norway Chess 2014.

11.d5 Karjakin tried 11.♘g5, but with the text-move Magnus follows in the footsteps of Kramnik.

11...b5! Despite winning the game against Kramnik after the sequence 11...♘d7 12.c4 ♛a3 13.♗e2 ♗xf3 14.♗xf3 ♗d4!, Grischuk decides to avoid Magnus' preparation (!) and springs his new idea first.

12.♗e2

Critical might be to take the pawn on c5, but after 12.♗xc5 ♗xf3 13.gxf3 ♖c8 Black has compensation: 14.♗d4 ♗xd4 15.♛xd4 ♘d7 is just fine for Black, and 14.♗b4 ♛c7 leaves an uncoordinated impression from White. So Magnus instead reverts to common sense development.

12...♘d7 13.0-0

Peter Heine Nielsen and Magnus Carlsen have a quick check after the game. Was this a King's Indian or a Grünfeld?

13...♗xf3?!

After the game, Grischuk said that 11...b5 was old prep and that his recollection was that the computers back then said Black was better, meaning he was in 'refutation mode', playing principled decisions to expose the flaws of the White position. Modern engines, however, have modified their views, and think Black is fine, but no more.

14.♗xf3

Common sense, but 14.gxf3, followed by either f4 or h4, has definite potential, too.

14...c4 15.♗e2

One does not have to be AlphaZero to suggest 15.h4! here, because Stockfish prefers it, too! Magnus, however, first sets up a broad centre, and then builds up his attack on the wing.

15...♖fd8?!

As on move 13, Grischuk is too stuck on the idea of having a good position, so he plays too ambitiously, aiming for rooks on d8 and c8.

15...♖ad8! was more to the point, caring about defensive details, e.g. that vacating the a8-square would remove the rook from being targeted by the f3-bishop, but especially that leaving the other rook on f8 would have it defend against, and counter, the upcoming assault on the f-file. This is especially relevant in the line 16.f4 ♛a3 17.♗f3, in which 17...♘c5 18.e5 f6! makes a considerable difference to the game.

16.f4!

The big difference now is that 16...♛a3 17.♗f3 ♘c5 18.e5 f6 19.d6!, hitting a8, is possible, when after 19...♖ac8 20.♗d5+ e6 21.f5! White's attack just crashes through.

16...♘b6 17.♗f3 ♛a3 18.h4!?

In a later interview Magnus mentioned AlphaZero and Daniil Dubov as his current chess heroes! One does see the inspiration, with optimistic and untamed long-term aggression. There is no immediate threat, and Black's counterplay might even get there first, but White does aim for the king, and will hit substantially harder than Black's smaller threats when the attack arrives at the intended target.

18...e6

Here 18...b4!? aims at distracting White, but he will just ignore it with 19.h5!. 19...♗xc3 20.♕f2 might win Black a pawn and create two passed pawns on the queenside, but White couldn't care less, since he intends to finish the game way before such things become decisive. After 20...♗g7 21.hxg6 hxg6 both 22.f5 ♖f8 23.e5!? and 22.♗g4 b3 23.f5 g5 24.f6!? exf6 25.axb3 cxb3 26.♖c7 give White a very promising attack.

19.h5!

Grischuk's problem is that 19...exd5 20.e5! makes things even worse, because Black gets another useless pawn, while speeding up White's attack, with ♗d4, f5, ♗g4, etc., being the next wave of attack.

19...♘a4 20.hxg6

Not h6! this time but hxg6. Yes, White has spent two tempi opening the h-file, apparently to little effect. It does weaken the g6-pawn, which will later be subject to a possible attack, but as we'll soon see, the open h-file is very relevant.

20...hxg6 21.f5

21...exf5

Yu Yangyi did very well in the Armageddon games, prevailing in four of the five he playe

21...♗xc3 obviously is critical, but apart from just sidestepping with his queen, White has the even more powerful exchange sac 22.♖xc3!, when White's attack becomes unstoppable: 22...♕xc3 23.♕f2. Now 24.♗d4 is a deadly threat, and 23...♕g7 24.fxe6 fxe6 25.♗g4! highlights why the open h-file makes such a difference, ♗(x)e6+, followed by ♕h4+, being the deadly threat.

22.exf5 ♕d6 23.♗f4 ♕b6+ 24.♔h1 gxf5 25.d6!

Grischuk has staved off immediate defeat, but against the next wave of attack he is helpless.

25...♖ab8 26.♗d5 ♘c5 27.♗g3

♘e6 28.♖xf5 Now ♖xf7 is a threat.
28...♖xd6 29.♗xd6 ♕xd6 30.♕e3 ♕b6 31.♕f3 ♖f8 32.♖f1 ♘d8 33.♖h5 ♕c7 34.♕e4

And here, fittingly, the open h-file has the final word. Mate on h7 is unavoidable, so Grischuk resigned.

■ ■ ■

Besides Magnus, Yu and Aronian were the main beneficiaries of the new format. Yu also won almost every Armageddon he played, while Ding Liren, China's number one, lost almost all of his. Yu, who was the replacement of Anish Giri, impressed no-one in the blitz, where he scored only 3½ points, but in the Armageddons he won four of his five games. An interesting pawn ending arose in the Armageddon game against Caruana.

Yu Yangyi
Fabiano Caruana
Stavanger 2019 (5, Armageddon)

position after 57.♔c6

As the black king's position indicates, there has been a lot of checking around with no time on the clock but the two-second increments. Yu was about to blitz out another check, but then suddenly stopped for a few seconds. Was it time to liquidate? **58.♕xb5+** The computers think it's winning, but it actually isn't. **58...♕xb5 59.♗xb5+ ♔xb5 60.♗xe3 fxe3 61.♔f1 ♔c4 62.♔e2 ♔d4 63.g3**

63...♔d5? After 63...g4! 64.fxg4 hxg4 65.h4 ♔e4 Black is saved, as 66.h5 ♔f5 67.♔xe3 ♔g5 68.♔e4 ♔xh5 69.♔f5 ♔h6 70.♔xg4 ♔g6 is a classical draw. **64.♔xe3 ♔e5 65.f4+ ♔f5 66.♔f3** 1-0. With the black pawn on h7 these endgames can be drawn, but certainly not in this way.

In the classical games, Yu was also a colourful player, with only five draws. He lost the crucial game against Magnus, but in the last round he recovered by beating Mamedyarov.

NOTES BY
Yu Yangyi

Yu Yangyi
Shakhriyar Mamedyarov
Stavanger 2019 (9)
Scotch Opening, Four Knights Variation

This game was played in the last round. Before the round I thought that the classical game might well end in a draw and that we would then play an Armageddon game. But things went differently.
1.e4 e5 2.♘f3 ♘c6 3.♘c3 ♘f6 4.d4 exd4 5.♘xd4 ♗b4 6.♘xc6 bxc6 7.♗d3 d5 8.exd5 0-0 9.0-0 ♗g4 10.f3 ♗h5

11.♗g5
One of the two main options in this position. The other one is 11.dxc6, as I played against Aronian in Round 7 of this tournament and which after 11...♕d4+ 12.♔h1 ♗xc3 13.bxc3 ♕xc3 14.♗f4 ♕xc6 15.♕d2 ♗g6 16.♖ac1 ♖fd8 17.♖fe1 a5 18.♗e5 led to an approximately equal position (½-½, 31).
11...♕d6 12.♗xf6
A new move I had found in my analysis. I know that someone had played 12.♕e1 here.
12...♕xf6 13.♘e4 ♕xb2 14.dxc6 ♗g6 15.♔h1 ♕d4 16.♕e2

16...♖fe8?! This is a slight mistake by Black. I think that after 16...♕d5!? the position is basically equal. Also interesting was 16...♖ae8!? 17.♖ad1 ♔h8.
17.♖ad1 ♕e5?!
Not a good move; better was 17...♔h8!?.

18.♗c4! A forceful move, clearing the d-file for the rook.
Less convincing was 18.c3 ♗xc3 19.f4 ♕a5 20.f5 ♗xf5 21.♖xf5 ♕xf5 22.♘xc3 ♕c5 23.♕c2 ♖ad8 24.♖f1, with unclear play.

18...♖ad8? A clear mistake. He should have tried 18...♔h8, when after 19.c3 White is only marginally better. Less attractive was 18...♗xe4 19.fxe4, and the vulnerability of f7 gives White an advantage.
19.♖d7!

Here I felt that I was in the driver's seat and had chances to win the game. **19...♖xd7 20.cxd7 ♖d8 21.♖d1 ♔f8** After 21...c6, 22.♗b3 is good for White.
22.c3

22...♗a3 Maybe a better defence was 22...♗d6 23.♘xd6 cxd6 24.♕xe5 dxe5 25.g4 ♗c2 26.♖d5 ♗a4 27.♖xe5, when White has an endgame with an extra pawn, but Black at least eliminates the pawn on d7.

23.♖d5 ♕e7 24.♗b5 ♗d6
24...♕e6 25.♗c4 f5 does not solve anything, because of 26.♕xc7 ♗e7 27.♖e5 ♕xa2 28.♕xd8+! ♗xd8 29.♖e8+ ♔f7 30.♗c4+, and White wins.
25.c4!

Now White is winning, because the d7-pawn is simply too strong.
25...a6
Perhaps his best try was 25...f5, but after 26.c5 fxe4 27.cxd6 cxd6 28.♕e3

Black's position remains problematic.
26.♗a4 ♗xe4 27.♕xe4 ♕xe4 28.fxe4 f6 29.♖a5 ♖b8 30.g3

And because the a6-pawn will fall and White's technical task is not too problematic anymore, Black resigned. I was very happy to win this game, because it brought me a shared 2nd-3rd place. I hope that in the future I will play more good games and have good results.

∎ ∎ ∎

Levon Aronian also profited from the new format. He lost the Armageddon against the World Champion, but his general Armageddon score was good, with five wins and two losses. This yielded him third place, despite only scoring 50 percent in the classical games. Still, he remained critical: 'My play in the Armageddons was terrible. I was not focused at all, I didn't have the motivation. It's kind of strange. But closer to the end I got myself together. At some point I was saying, oh, how unfair that we have to play this, and then I said to myself, OK, time to concentrate and just do your job, which I think I managed closer to the end.'

NOTES BY
Levon Aronian

Levon Aronian
Wesley So
Stavanger 2019 (6, Armageddon)
English Opening, Smyslov System

1.c4 e5 2.g3 ♞f6 3.♘c3 ♝b4 4.e4

A wonderful idea of Vladimir Georgiev's, first tried in the early 2000s and made popular by Carlsen's recent victory against Caruana in the World Championship tie-breaker. The main difference between this idea and 4.♗g2 0-0 5.e4 is that White is keeping the bishop on f1 if Black takes on c3.

4...0-0 5.♘ge2 ♞c6
A solid line. Despite White having a grip over the centre, there are active plans for Black, e.g. the ...a6/...b5 thrust or ...f5 ideas, either immediately or after some simplifications.

6.♗g2 ♝c5 7.0-0 d6

8.d3 Here 8.h3 is more common, but I had a different idea.
8...♗g4 Very logical. Black's control of the dark squares should give him good counterplay.
9.♔h1
Keeping the h3-square for future use. Now Black has to take, otherwise the point behind ...♗g4 is lost.
9...♗xe2 10.♕xe2
10.♘xe2 required the calculation of 10...♘g4, which is not desired in an Armageddon game.
10...♘d4 The next three moves are natural and good.
11.♕d1 c6 12.f4 h6 13.♘a4
Creating a positional threat.

13...♝b4
The most natural move, but perhaps not the best one. White threatened to trap the d4-knight by taking on c5 and playing f5, but Black should probably still go for it, hoping for quick counterplay via ...b5. The d4-knight does not have many moves,

but controls way too many squares.
14.a3 ♝a5 15.♗e3 b5 16.cxb5 cxb5 17.♘c3 ♝b6 18.♖c1

So far, the game is balanced, and both sides are making decent moves.
18...a6 19.♗h3 This looks like the right move, but 19.g4 was a better try.
19...♖e8 20.g4
Not a bad move for a blitz game.

20...♘e6
A tactical oversight. The solution to the problem was 20...exf4 21.♖xf4, and now the simple but great move 21...♝a7, with the idea of exchanging more pieces via ...♘e6. Note that 21...♘e6 is bad in view of 22.♗xb6 ♕xb6 23.♖xf6 gxf6 24.♕d2, with a very dangerous attack.
21.♗xb6 ♕xb6

Mate in one is a rare occurrence in grandmaster games, but so are many things we saw in the Armageddons...

22.g5 Probably missed by Wesley.
22...hxg5 The next three moves are forced. **23.♗xe6 fxe6 24.fxg5 ♘h7**

25.♕g4
I spent about three minutes (out of seven!) looking for a forced win, and failed. The win was to be achieved in slow fashion: 25.g6 ♘f6 26.♕f3, followed by ♕h3/♘d1, and after the transfer of the knight to g4 Black loses the last defender.
25...♕e3 26.h4 At least, I thought, I'll keep the black knight locked up.
26...♖f8 There was nothing wrong with taking on d3, but the game move is more forcing.
27.g6 Not a good move, but it got the job done.
27...♖xf1+ I had missed that after 27...♘f6 28.♕xe6+ ♔h8 29.♕f5 ♘g8 the knight reroutes to h6, giving Black at least a safe position.
28.♖xf1 ♘f8 29.h5

This is a big achievement. Now the knight on f8 is very passive, and I can spend less time on my moves.
29...♕xd3 30.♔g2 White needs to consolidate and slowly transfer the c3-knight to a better spot.
30...♕d2+ 31.♖f2 The next few moves were played almost instantly.
31...♕e3 32.♘d1 ♕c1 33.♕f3 ♕g5+ 34.♔f1 ♕e7
34...♕f4 was a better try, but 34...♕e7 looked OK as well.
35.♔e2 b4 36.a4 A good move that keeps the black rook passive.

36...♘d7?
A blunder in a difficult position. Black should have just sat tight.
37.♕f7+ ♕xf7 38.♖xf7 ♘c5
38...♘f6 loses beautifully after 39.h6 ♘h5 40.h7+ ♔h8 41.♘f2 ♘f4+ 42.♖xf4 exf4 43.♘h3, and ♘g5-f7+ cannot be stopped.
39.♘f2 ♖f8 40.♖c7 b3

41.♘g4?
A blunder on my part, but luck was on my side.
41.h6 would have won on the spot.
41...♘xe4 42.h6 ♘g3+ 43.♔e1 ♘f5 44.hxg7 ♘xg7 45.♘h6+ ♔h8 46.♖a7

I had seen that I could take on a6 and that after ...♘f5 I could go ♖a7, since I had the g7 check after ...♘xh6.
46...♘f5
Mate in one is a rare occurrence in grandmaster games, but so are many things we saw in the Armageddons...
47.♖h7
Mate.

■ ■ ■

Aronian had this to say about the new format: 'I cannot say I dislike the Armageddon format. It feels a bit unfair because of the points, I think you should get more points in the classical part, but other than that it's a lot of fun. I wish we had had some time after move 40, some 10 minutes, just to go to the bathroom. And maybe bigger increments (than 10 seconds). I think there are zillions of ideas. If the organizers get the players involved, we can come up with lots and lots of interesting ideas to enhance the game. And I hope there will be more FischerRandom, because when you're talking about stopping the draws, there is nothing more efficient.'

In his classical game against Mamedyarov, Aronian impressed with some advanced positional and tactical judgements.

Shakhriyar Mamedyarov
Levon Aronian
Stavanger 2019 (3)

position after 19.♗c4

19...♖d8! The critical test. 19...bxc5 20.♕e5 gives White what he wants with two great bishops and active play. **20.♗xe6+**

20...♕xe6 20...♔h8 21.♗d7! doesn't work for Black neither after 21...bxc5 22.♗a3! nor after 21...♖f7 22.c6 ♗xc6 23.♗xc6!. **21.♕xd8 ♖xd8 22.♖xd8+ ♔f7**

23.♖d1 23.cxb6 ♕f6 was the point, but the variation goes a bit further: 24.♖d4 c5 25.♗b2 cxd4 26.♗xd4 ♕c6 27.bxa7 could have been interesting, but for 27...g5! and breaking

up the long diagonal. **23...bxc5 24.♖e1 c4 25.♗d2**

25...g5! Essential! Black will soon dominate on the light squares. **26.♗c3 g4 27.fxg4 ♕e4 28.♖a2 ♕d3**

Levon Aronian was in a buoyant and talkative mood when he joined Judit Polgar in the international broadcast after yet another Armageddon win.

29.♗a1 The natural 29.♗d4 would have given Aronian the very challenging task to find 29...h5!. The point appears in the line 29...c3 30.♖c1 c5! 31.♗xc5 ♕d5 (or 31...♕c4), and now 32.♖f2! saves the day, since the bishop on c5 is taboo in view of the capture on f5. So, first the pressure on f5 has to be released. After 29...h5 30.gxh5 or 30.gxf5, 30...c3! the tricks work for Black. The position is all about getting the pawn down to c2 and cover it with the bishop on e4. **29...c3 30.♖f2 ♗e4 31.♖c1 c2**

0-1. White can't take any of the pawns without losing a rook: 32.♖cxc2 ♕d1+, 32.♖fxc2 ♕xe3+ and, finally, 32.gxf5 ♕d1+ 33.♖f1 ♕d2!.

Fair & Square

Arnold Schwarzenegger: 'I started [chess] when I was eight with my father; I had to play with him every day. When I went to America, I started playing over there with friends and people at the gym. It was always part of me.' *(The iconic actor and former Governor of California, speaking of his passion for chess at the opening of the Arnold Chess Classic games in mid-May in Johannesburg, South Africa)*

David Norwood: 'Masters don't calculate more. They calculate better.'

Sergey Belavenets: 'Repeating moves in an ending can be very useful. Apart from the obvious gain of time on the clock, one notices that the side with the advantage gains psychological benefit.' *(The early 20th century Soviet master and Red Army soldier, who was killed in action during the Battle of Staraya Russa in 1942)*

Juan Fernandez: 'For a long time we were not aware of the enormous importance that involved organizing the world's most important tournament. Chess put us on the Spanish and world map. Today it becomes fashionable again for its great social and educational value, and we see with pride that we put the first stone.' *(The longtime Linares mayor in the Spanish newspaper El Pais)*

Georges Perec: 'Chess is a fathead and feudal game.' *(The 20th century French novelist, filmmaker and essayist)*

Ronnie O'Sullivan: 'This guy is a genius, saw a documentary on him – unbelievable.' *(Tweeted in mid-May by the five-time snooker World Champion, after watching a Eurosport cable TV profile on Magnus Carlsen during their coverage of the FIDE Moscow GP)*

Magnus Carlsen: 'If I ever do something else, I'll make sure that I spend a lot of time on it and be humble. I know how much time I've spent on chess to be at this level and I know how much it's about hard work to be good at anything. I respect people who work hard.' *(In an interview before a simultaneous exhibition in Copenhagen)*

Courtney Love: 'It's the horsey-shape piece that moves in an L shape. It's what makes chess complicated, and why stupid people can't play chess. Go play checkers! Knights are the first piece you look at. They elevate the game. No chess master wants to lose her knights.'

Alexander Grischuk: 'Draw is better than losing and worse than winning.' *(Interviewed after his uneventful opening game draw with Sergey Karjakin at the Moscow FIDE Grand Prix)*

Kateryna Lagno: 'If you lose a game, it's better just to try to forget about it because there is a new game tomorrow. If you cannot stand the pressure you should not play chess.' *(Alexander Grischuk's better half interviewed during the Women's Candidates Tournament in Kazan)*

Edwyn Anthony: 'The game of Chess stands at the head of sedentary pastimes.' *(The Victorian era founder – along with Lord Randolph Churchill – and President of the Oxford University Chess Club)*

Jacob Aagaard: 'The things you overlook in your long calculations will seldom be as important as the move you overlooked at the start.' *(On calculating long variations, in his book 'Excelling at Chess Calculation')*

Pietro Carrera: 'Who will deny that the mind is awakened and excited to victory by ingenious positions?' *(The Italian priest, historian and chess player, whom the Sicilian Defence was named after in his 1617 book, 'The Game of Chess')*

Raymond Rozman: 'And we've kept with his collecting habit and we now have the world's largest collection of chess material, period. It is an interesting, fascinating little world.' *(The Special Collections Librarian at Cleveland Public Library in a mid-June profile for ABC 5 TV News on the John G. White Chess Collection)*

As usual, lots of unusual stuff happened in Caruana's games. In the classical game against Anand, Caruana conducted a brilliant attack – almost.

Fabiano Caruana
Vishy Anand
Stavanger 2019 (7)

position after 28...♕b4

Fabiano Caruana had a poor start losing his first three Armageddons, but the American fought back and he was certainly pleased by his last-round Armageddon win against Magnus Carlsen.

I was a guest commentator for TV2 this day and could see the computers screaming out 29.♗xg6, winning, but would Caruana see it? He was thinking and thinking, despite having only about 10 minutes left.
29.♗xg6! Tjoho! Big enthusiasm in the studio when Caruana finally went for it.
29...♕xe1+ 30.♔h2 Now it was Anand's turn to think. **30...♖d5** He puts up the most resilient defence.

Tjoho! Big enthusiasm in the studio when Caruana finally went for it.

31.♖c1! Caruana didn't seem to be surprised and played the best move almost instantly. **31...♖g5** A last desperate attempt.

32.♕f3 Oh no! 32.♗f7+ ♔h8 33.♗xg5 ♕e5 34.♗f4 ♕d5 35.♗h6 is such a simple and obvious win, but somehow Caruana starts messing it up. **32...♕xe6 33.♕xa8+ ♔g7 34.♗d3**

34...♕d5!
The game isn't over after all.
35.♕xd5 ♖xd5 36.♗xa6 c4 37.♗xc4 ♖xa5

The crisis is over for Anand, and eventually Caruana had to fight for the draw. In the Armageddon just after, however, Caruana didn't fail and won a great game.

Age as a factor
Caruana started horribly, losing his three first Armageddons, but recovered by winning the three last, including the win against Magnus. One would expect Maxime Vachier-Lagrave to thrive with playoffs like these, but he, too, scored only a relatively bleak 50 percent in the Armageddons, while Wesley So said he

was happy with the same score. Grischuk mentioned age as a factor when things get speedy. Anand, aged 49, seems to be the only one of my generation still maintaining his level. With 'minus one' in the classical games and 50 percent in the Armageddon, Anand was keeping up. His only loss in the classical game was due to a big blunder, a typical phenomenon that comes with getting close to 50?

Vishy Anand
Shakhriyar Mamedyarov
Stavanger 2019 (2)

position after 33...e4

34.fxg4? Anand has misplayed an equal position and is now worse, but blundering like this is extremely rare for him.
34...♗c8 0-1.

Back in the 1980s I remember being annoyed by Ulf Andersson's ultra-solid play and tried hard to get him out of his style to beat him, only to find out how enormously strong he was, even in complicated positions. Garry Kasparov writes about a similar experience when playing old Tigran Petrosian. The modern-day version is perhaps Vishy Anand. He is extremely solid and sometimes it can be a bit boring watching his games. However, against an ambitious Ding Liren we got a chance to see what Vishy is capable of. It started with an incredibly complicated classical game of 107 moves. The Armageddon was shorter, but no less spectacular.

NOTES BY
Vishy Anand

Vishy Anand
Ding Liren
Stavanger 2019 (4, Armageddon)
Giuoco Piano

Before my encounter with Ding Liren, my second Gajewski and I had prepared two ideas: one that I used in the classical game (a very complex line), and one that he told me I could play on move 12. And that was the end of that part of the preparation. In the faster time-controls, the most important is often that you know what you are doing.
1.e4 e5 2.♘f3 ♘c6 3.♗c4 ♗c5 4.0-0 ♘f6 5.d3 0-0 6.c3 d6 7.♖e1 a5 8.h3 h6 9.♘bd2 ♗e6 10.♗b5 ♕b8 11.♘f1 ♕a7

Now, in the classical game, I had played 12.d4, and that game had ended in a draw.
12.♕d2 This was played by Dominguez. It stops 12...♗xf2+ and allows White to continue with his plan of bishop takes c6 and d4. If you play 12.♖e2 to defend f2, the rook is slightly clumsily placed, and after 12.♗e3 pieces get exchanged.
There are all kinds of small details. Suppose, for instance, that Black would continue 12...a4. In that

case, after 13.♗xc6 bxc6 14.d4 exd4 15.cxd4, he would not have 15...♗b4. And if White plays d4 and the pawns are exchanged on d4, White might also put his queen on f4.
12...♖ad8 13.♘g3 ♘e7 14.d4 ♗b6 15.♕c2

The rook is already on e1 and my bishops will go to e3 and d3, and that's a very pleasant edge.
15...♘g6 16.♗e3 c6 17.♗d3 ♖fe8 18.♕d2

Now that the bishop is on e3, the queen returns to d2. Here I remembered a game I played against Hikaru Nakamura at the Champions Showdown in St. Louis in 2016, where the structure was essentially the same, with some slight differences. There I also played ♕d2, but I had missed a decisive attack with ♗xh6, as I discovered when I returned to my room afterwards.

This time I was very confident that this was very dangerous for Black, and I didn't hesitate a second.

18...d5 I don't know if he can play 18...♔h7 19.♘f5 exd4 (after 19...♝g8 20.g4 the play is very pleasant for White) 20.♗xh6 dxc3. White has 21.♕g5!, with an initiative that should be winning for White.

19.♗xh6 This time I was very confident that this was very dangerous for Black, and I didn't hesitate a second.

19...dxe4? A clear mistake. The alternative was 19...exd4 and now:

– 20.e5? is just worse for White, and after 20...dxc3 (or 20...♘e4) he will be lost.

– The correct answer would have been 20.cxd4 dxe4 21.♘xe4 ♗xd4 22.♗g5, and here Black's disadvantage would have been much smaller.

20.♘xe4 ♘xe4

Vishy Anand knew exactly what he was doing when he sacrificed his bishop against Ding Liren. And yes, he had seen the spectacular killer 27.♗h8! way before he played it.

21.♖xe4?
This is simply a mistake, especially since the straightforward 21.♗xe4 exd4 22.♕g5 (and White should be winning) was available. In fact, 21.♖xe4? reflects my poor play in this tournament.

21...♗d5 22.♖g4 e4
22...♗xf3 23.gxf3 would be very strong for White,

23.♘h4 I went ahead with my plan without much calculation.

23...exd3

24.♘f5
I had seen that 24.♘xg6 fxg6 25.♖xg6 ♖d7 26.♗xg7 ♖xg7 27.♖xg7+ ♔xg7 28.♕g5+ would lead to a draw, but

obviously I was not aiming for that. 24.♘f5 is a good gamble, as 24...♖e2 is not at all easy to play or to calculate, but I didn't see it as a gamble at this point.

24...♗e6?
He played this quickly. Here the big move was 24...♖e2. I think Black can make this move even without seeing all its consequences, but he would have to find several difficult moves. Here are the key lines: 24...♖e2 25.♕g5 (after 25.♕xd3 ♕a6 26.♕g3 gxh6 27.♖xg6+ fxg6 28.♕xg6+ ♔f8 Black is winning) 25...d2 (White would be fine after 25...♗e6 26.♗xg7 ♗xf5 27.♕h6 f6 28.♖xg6) 26.♗xg7

ANALYSIS DIAGRAM

and here Black faces a tough choice.
– One way is 26...♕b8 27.♖f1 (after
27.f4 ♖de8! is essential) 27...♖e1
28.♕xd2 ♖xf1+ 29.♔xf1 ♕h2!, with
an advantage for Black.
– After 26...♗c7 27.♗e5 ♖e1+ 28.♔h2
♗xe5+ 29.dxe5 the critical move is
29...♕xf2, allowing White to take a
rook with check, 30.♕xd8+, when after
30...♔h7 Black is still winning.
All this is very difficult, but the upshot
is that Black is better after 24...♖e2.

25.♗xg7

A very nice move to make.

25...♗xf5 26.♕h6 ♖e6 27.♗h8!

A move I had seen from afar, around
the time I played 23.♘h4. Sometimes
these moves do not pop up in your
vision no matter what you do, and
sometimes, like here, they turn up
instantly. Black can still stave off the
mate for some moves but it's unavoidable, so Black resigned.

■ ■ ■

The three that suffered most in the
Armageddon were Ding Liren, Mamedyarov and Grischuk. Ding started off
well, though, with a brilliant Armageddon win against Wesley So.

NOTES BY
Ding Liren

Ding Liren
Wesley So
Stavanger 2019 (1, Armageddon)
Queen's Gambit, Exchange Variation

So far, my results in Armageddon
games have been one win and nine
losses. Here is my first and only
Armageddon win for the moment.
**1.c4 e6 2.♘c3 d5 3.d4 ♘f6
4.cxd5 ♘xd5 5.e4 ♘xc3 6.bxc3
c5 7.♖b1 ♗e7 8.♘f3 0-0 9.♗c4
a6 10.a4 ♕c7 11.♗e2**

This and the next moves have all been
seen before. Two years ago, against
Kramnik, I played 11.♗d3 here.
**11...b6 12.0-0 cxd4 13.cxd4 ♗b7
14.♗d3 ♘c6 15.♖b3**

This move I had prepared for the
Candidates tournament in Berlin
last year. I was very happy to find this
move. The computer underestimates
its power, but it allows White to create
very strong threats that are difficult
to handle with this time-control.
The point is that at some point, the

rook can be switched to the kingside,
but at the same time the b1-square is
vacated for the light-squared bishop,
while the other bishop can go to b2.
15...♘a5 16.♖b2
This is another point. From here, the
rook will go to d2, where we will see it
is also quite useful.
16...♘c6 17.♖d2
In case of 17.♖c2, Black would go
17...♕d7, which would be annoying
for White.
17...♖fd8 18.♗b2 ♖ac8 19.d5

A good move. I could not see any
other useful moves here and decided
to attack immediately.
19...♘b4
Because after 19...exd5 20.exd5 ♘b4
White would have 21.♗e4.
20.♗b1 I could also have played
20.dxe6, but I felt that after 20...
fxe6 my attacking chances might be
reduced, and I wanted to keep the
tension and sacrifice the pawn.
20...exd5 21.e5 g6
A strong defensive move.

22.♖e1 A small inaccuracy. I should
have played 22.e6, when after 22...
fxe6 23.♘d4 e5, 24.♕g4 (24...exd4
25.♕xd4) is very strong.

22...d4 A good move, giving back the pawn.

23.e6 23.♘xd4? would fail to 23...♗g5.

23...f6? This is a mistake. He should have taken the pawn, 23...fxe6 24.♖xe6, and the position is unclear (after 24.♘xd4 there is again 24...♗g5).

24.♘xd4 ♘c6 25.♘f5! I spent about two minutes on this nice move.

25...♖xd2 After 25...gxf5 my plan was to play 26.♖d7, which is a very nice move to make. Actually, 26.♕h5 is even stronger: 26...♖xd2 27.♕f7+ ♔h8 28.♗xf5, and White wins.

26.♘xe7+

After the removal of the bishop the black kingside is very vulnerable, especially on the dark squares.

26...♕xe7 27.♕xd2 ♔g7

After 27...♘e5 I have 28.♗a2.

28.♕f4 Eyeing the f6-pawn and preparing h4.

28...♖f8 29.h4

29...♗c8 Maybe he should have tried to create some counterplay here with 29...♕b4 30.♕c7+ ♔g8 31.♖f1 ♕xb2, but now, after 32.♕xb7 ♘d4 33.♕d7 ♕d2 34.♗a2 ♕xa2 35.e7, White is winning anyway.

30.h5

30...♘e5

After 30...♗xe6 the simplest is 31.hxg6 hxg6 32.♕e4 (or the even stronger 32.♕g3). Now the rest is very simple.

31.♖xe5 fxe5 32.♕xe5+ ♔h6 33.hxg6 hxg6 34.♕h2+ ♔g5 35.♕g3+ Black resigned.

■ ■ ■

However, Ding lost all his next six Armageddon encounters. His classical play was of the usual solid standard with two wins and seven draws. He was particularly proud of the game he won against Caruana.

NOTES BY
Ding Liren

**Ding Liren
Fabiano Caruana**
Stavanger 2019 (3)
Queen's Pawn Opening

In the third round, I faced Fabiano Caruana. My previous results against him were bad, especially in classical chess, in which I had not won a single game.

1.d4 ♘f6 2.g3

I chose this rare line, which I had also played against Anish Giri at the Batumi Olympiad, when I got a good

My previous results against Caruana were bad, especially in classical chess, in which I had not won a single game.

position (½-½, 42). The point is that you give Black many options.

2...e6 He chooses to delay ...d5.

3.♗g2 c5 4.♘f3 cxd4 5.0-0 ♕c7 This came as a big surprise. Black is ready to play a Sicilian Paulsen structure.

6.♘xd4 a6

7.b3 A nice idea. I want to go c4. After 7.e4 ♘c6 we would have a Paulsen position, which I am not too familiar with.

7...d5

Again not what I had expected, and also a slight mistake, since it allows me to sacrifice a pawn immediately.

8.c4 dxc4 9.♗b2

Here I was very happy with my position. My opponent now thought for a very long time.

9...cxb3

I was mainly considering 9...e5 10.♘f3 ♘c6 (if 10...e4 11.♘fd2 e3 12.♘xc4 exf2+ 13.♔h1, with good attacking chances) 11.bxc4 (the computer also suggests 11.♘bd2) 11...♗e6 12.♕a4 (also strong is 12.♘g5 ♗xc4 13.♘d2) 12...♘d7 13.♘g5 ♗f5 14.♘c3 ♘c5 15.♘d5 ♕d8 16.♕d1, and was not completely sure about the position, but the computer assesses it as better for White.

10.♕xb3

10...♘c6

Again not the move I had anticipated, and it turns out to be a very big mistake.

I had expected 10...♘bd7, when I had planned 11.♖c1 (better is 11.♘d2 and just develop with ♖ac1, ♖fd1 and ♘c4, and White has long-term compensation for the pawn) 11...♗c5

Ding Liren during the visit to the school competition. The Chinese number one was relieved that he finally managed to beat Fabiano Caruana in a classical game.

12.♘c3, and here, after 12...♗xd4 13.♘d5, White is winning, but Black has 12...♕b6 13.♘a4 ♕xb3 14.♘xb3 ♗e7 15.♘a5 ♖b8, and holds.

11.♘xc6 bxc6 12.♗xf6 gxf6

13.♕c3

I guess my opponent had missed this move. I get back the pawn with a better pawn structure and nice attacking chances. With accurate play, White is positionally winning. I was very pleased with the outcome of the opening, but as it turned out, the game had only just begun.

13...♗d7 14.♕xf6 ♖g8 15.♘c3 ♖g6 16.♕f3

Maybe I could have gone for more

with 16.♕h4. At least it gains a tempo.

16...♗e7 17.♖ac1 ♔f8 18.♘e4

I want to transfer the knight to c5 and then maybe to d3, and then e5, followed by f4.

18...♗e8

19.♘c5 This is actually a pawn sacrifice. It's a good move, but it requires a forceful continuation, and after the game I regretted that I had rushed things. I could have played slowly with first 19.♖c2 and only then ♘c5, but I saw no need to do that.

19...♕a5

He decides he doesn't want to stay passive and goes for the pawn.

20.♕e3 ♕xa2 21.♗e4
This is a slight inaccuracy.
Better was 21.h4, threatening h5, and
after 21...♕b2 I have 22.♘d3. The
pawn on h4 also covers the g5-square.
21...♖g7 22.♖c2 ♕a5 23.♖b1

This was the position I had in mind
when I sacrificed the pawn. I threaten
to go 24.♖b7 and Black has a cramped
position.
23...♕c7
A very natural move. Actually, the
computer suggests 23...h5, but this is
very risky.
24.♕f3
Here I realized that after 24.♖b7 ♕d6
it is hard to launch an attack.
24...♔g8
Now I think that 24...♕d6 would
have been better.
25.♖b7 ♕d6

26.♗d3 The right move, threatening 27.♘e4. My first intention was
to play 26.♔g2, but this is not the end
of the story, because in fact 26.♔g2 is
not good, not because of 26...a5, but
because of 26...f5 when, after 27.♗d3
♔h8, Black will hold.
After 26...a5 I have 27.♗xh7+ ♖xh7
28.♘e4, and now 28...♕d8 runs into
29.♖d2 and 28...♕a3 into 29.♖c3.
But he has 28...♕e5 29.♖xe7 f5
30.♖xh7 fxe4, and I thought this was
winning for Black. But the computer
gives a great resource: 31.♕b3, and
now it's White who is winning:
31...♔xh7 (or 31...♖b8 32.♖b7)
32.♕b7+.
26...♗d8 After 26...a5 White plays
27.♘e4 ♕d8 28.♖d2, with many
threats, e.g. 28...♖b8 29.♘f6+ ♗xf6
30.♗xh7+ ♖xh7 31.♖xd8, and White
is winning.
27.♘e4 ♕e5 28.♖c5

28...♕d4 This turns out to be a
big mistake. He should have played
28...♕a1+ 29.♔g2 (29.♖b1 ♕d4, and
my rook is not placed as well as on
b7), when 29...f5 is a very important
resource for Black.
29.♖c4 First I repeated moves to get
closer to the time-control on move
40. **29...♕e5 30.♖c5 ♕d4**

31.♕f4 Here, instead of the text-
move, I had the very strong 31.♗c4,

removing the bishop from d3 and preventing ...f5, when all my pieces are well placed and my opponent cannot attack them. Next I will chase away his queen with e3 and then play ♘d6, and White is winning.

31...a5 This allows me to grab a piece. I had mainly focused on 31...f5, when I have 32.♖c4 ♕d5 33.♘c3 ♕a5 34.♖xg7+ ♔xg7, and my position is not as good as I thought during the game. Black has good chances to survive.

32.♖b8 ♖xb8 33.♕xb8

With the deadly threat of 34.♘d6.

33...♔f8

The point is that after 33...♕d7 White has 34.♖xa5 ♗xa5 35.♘f6+.

34.♘d6 ♗e7 35.♘xe8 ♕xc5

35...♔xe8 is met by 36.♖xc6.

And 35...♕xg3+ doesn't help either after 36.hxg3 ♕xc5 37.♘f6, and here the knight is well placed and may even grab a pawn.

36.♘xg7 a4

37.g4 A risky move that yields Black some chances to survive.

Better was 37.♕a8 a3 38.♗xh7 and just ignore his threats: 38...♕c1+ 39.♔g2 ♕b2 40.♕xc6 ♕xg7 (or 40...

a2 41.♕e8+ ♔d6 42.♕xd8+ ♔c5 43.♕e7+, and the threats against the black king are decisive) 41.♕c5+ ♔e8 42.♗d3 f5 43.♕xa3, and White is winning.

I was only considering 37.♕b7+ ♔f8 38.♕a8 ♔xg7 39.♕xd8 a3, but I missed 40.♕a8 ♕b4 41.♕a6, which is also winning for White.

37...a3 38.♕b3 ♗b6 39.e3

39...♕g5 Here he should have played 39...a2 40.♕xa2 ♕c3 41.♘f5+ (41.♕b1 doesn't work because of 41...♕xg7 42.♕xb6 ♕xg4+) 41...exf5 42.♗xf5, when White has good chances to win, but there is still work to do.

40.♘h5 Played after a long think.

40.♕xa3+ runs into 40...♗c5. And after 40.♘f5+ exf5 41.♕xa3+ c5 42.♗xf5 he has 42...h5.

So in the end I decided that keeping the knight was the best continuation.

40...♕xg4+ 41.♘g3 ♗c5 42.♔g2 h5 This is a bad move, but both of us were in serious time-trouble here. I had under five minutes left, and he had even less time.

43.h3

There was a simple win with 43.♕b7+ ♔f6 44.♕b8 h4 45.♕d8+ ♔g7 46.f3, when my pieces have such nice coordination that I even have mating threats.

43...♕g5 44.♔f1

It is difficult to lure chess players away from their laptops. Ding Liren and Yu Yangyi were the only participants that joined a relaxed boat ride on a luxury yacht on the last free day.

44...♛d5 I was very happy when he offered a queen swap, but actually it is not clear if White can win after this. I was worried about 44...♛h4, but I have 45.♘e4 ♛xh3+ 46.♔e1 ♛f5 47.♛c3! a2 48.♘xc5 a1♛+ 49.♛xa1 ♛xc5 50.♛a4, and the queen will go to h4 and I will win h5, which should be enough to win.

45.♛xd5 cxd5 The following moves were played very quickly.

46.♗b1 h4 47.♘e2 f5 48.♗f4 ♔f7 49.♗a2 ♗e7 50.♔e2 ♗f6 51.♔d3 ♗e5 52.♘g2 ♗f6 53.♘e1 ♗e7 54.♔c2 ♔f6 55.♘f3

55...f4 He decides to give up the pawn, which he could have kept with

55...♔g7. Whether this was a good idea only very deep analysis will show.

56.♘xh4 fxe3 57.fxe3 ♔g5 58.♘f3+ ♔f5 59.♔d3 White controls the position, but I have to find a way to break through.

59...♗c5 60.♘d4+ ♔e5 61.♘f3+ ♔f5 62.♔e2 ♔f6 63.♗b1

63...e5 This turns out to be the losing move, because it creates an additional weakness. It's not very likely that White can make progress after 63...♗d6 64.h4 ♗e7 65.h5 ♗f8 66.♔d3 ♗h6.

64.♗a2 e4 65.♘d4 ♔e5 66.♘b5 ♗e7 67.♗b3

A strong move that puts Black in a kind

of zugzwang. The black bishop cannot both defend the a3-pawn and keep the h-pawn in check.

67...♗c5 68.h4 d4 69.exd4+ ♗xd4 70.♘xa3 ♔f5 71.h5 ♔g5 72.♗f7

72...♔f4 This is a bad move. More resilient would have been 72...e3, when White has to start on a long plan to bring the bishop to e2.

73.♘c4 ♗g7 74.♗g6 ♗d4 75.♘d6 e3 76.♘f7 ♗g7 77.♗d3

And since nothing can stop the h-pawn from advancing, Black resigned. I was very happy with this long and hard fight.

■ ■ ■

Stavanger 2019					1	2	3	4	5	6	7	8	9	10		cat. XXII
																TPR
1	**Magnus Carlsen**	IGM	NOR	2875	*	2	½ 1	½ 0	½ 1	½ 1	½ 1	½ 1	½ 1	2	13½	2990
2	**Yu Yangyi**	IGM	CHN	2738	0	*	½ 0	½ 1	0	½ 1	½ 1	½ 1	2	2	10½	2888
3	**Levon Aronian**	IGM	ARM	2752	½ 0	½ 1	*	0	½ 1	½ 1	½ 0	½ 1	2	½ 1	10½	2886
4	**Fabiano Caruana**	IGM	USA	2819	½ 1	½ 0	2	*	½ 0	0	2	½ 1	½ 0	½ 1	10	2934
5	**Wesley So**	IGM	USA	2754	½ 0	2	½ 0	½ 1	*	½ 0	½ 1	½ 0	½ 1	½ 1	10	2941
6	**Ding Liren**	IGM	CHN	2805	½ 0	½ 0	½ 0	2	½ 1	*	½ 0	½ 0	2	½ 0	8½	2997
7	**Maxime Vachier-Lagrave**	IGM	FRA	2779	½ 0	½ 0	½ 1	0	½ 0	½ 1	*	½ 0	½ 1	½ 1	8	2831
8	**Vishy Anand**	IGM	IND	2767	½ 0	½ 0	½ 0	½ 0	½ 1	½ 1	½ 1	*	0	½ 1	8	2833
9	**Shakhriyar Mamedyarov**	IGM	AZE	2774	½ 0	0	0	½ 1	½ 0	0	½ 0	2	*	½ 0	5½	2785
10	**Alexander Grischuk**	GM	RUS	2775	0	0	½ 0	½ 0	½ 0	½ 1	½ 0	½ 0	½ 1	*	5½	2785
2 points for a win, ½ point for a draw plus 1 point for winning the Armageddon tiebreaker																

As pieces were falling everywhere, the first-round Armageddon game between Levon Aronian and Alexander Grischuk ended in chaos. The Russian was way ahead on the clock, but managed to lose on time. 'Extremely stupid and inexcusable.'

energy, but I didn't feel like using it for this tournament, especially when I started badly. At my age, you don't have so much of this emergency energy and I would rather use it on something else.'

Somehow it was not the chess results that disturbed his sleep, Grischuk claimed, but the fact that it was NBA games (American basketball) every third night till six or seven am.

It became even worse for Grischuk, with new disasters following. The worst one was the following:

Alexander Grischuk
Fabiano Caruana
Stavanger 2019 (6, Armageddon)

position after 16...d5

17.♗h6? ♗xh6 0-1.

Even after such a blunder Grischuk kept his calm and said he liked an online comment on ChessBomb or somewhere that he should learn that the queen cannot X-ray.

How the new format will be evaluated, we will see. Critical voices may ask whether this should be the future of chess. From the point of view of the action-hungry spectator it can be called a success and the Norwegians certainly enjoyed Magnus Carlsen's dominance in the Armageddon games; but then they are always happy when he wins. The organizers have promised to evaluate the experience, and it will be interesting to see what they come up with next year. ∎

However, the most remarkable Armageddon show came in the first round between Aronian and Grischuk. Aronian was perhaps slightly better on the board, but short of practice with the time-control, he had spent too much time and had lots of moves left to reach the increment phase after move 60. 'Actually, I thought we had made many more moves, about 10, than we in fact had', Grischuk explained, 'and it was impossible to look, you had to stand up (to see the number of moves played indicated on the overhead screens).'

Levon Aronian
Alexander Grischuk
Stavanger 2019 (1, Armageddon)

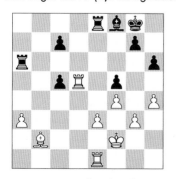

position after 34.a3

Aronian was down to 32 seconds while Grischuk had 62. However, Grischuk started hesitating. Decisions had to be made. 'This was extremely stupid on my part,' Grischuk commented, 'because I had just an automatic win on time. Any blitz player with experience, not necessarily a world-class player, 2100 is enough, you just play moves and you win on time. It was inexcusable.' Grischuk continued to feel uneasy, whereas Aronian finally started firing on all cylinders and blitzed out every move instantly.

At the end, both clocks were ticking down to zero. It was total chaos, and pieces were falling everywhere. It must have been horrible for Grischuk when his time ran out with one second left for Aronian. However, it was absolute fantastic TV.

Normally Grischuk is on top in these scrambles, but coming here almost straight from the FIDE Grand Prix in Moscow may have been a bit too much to ask. 'I didn't feel that I had so little energy, but apparently that was the case. It happens sometimes that you are very tired, but you don't feel it. I had no desire to play. Everybody has some emergency

Orchestrated manoeuvres in the dark

In early June *Clarin* reported on a secret mission of nine Argentinians, who, 37 years after the Falklands War between Argentina and Great Britain, had visited the islands to play chess. With the noble goal of fraternizing with their erstwhile enemies, the Argentinian newspaper touted. FIDE vice-president **NIGEL SHORT** sincerely doubts whether Gens Una Sumus was high on their agenda.

At the end of April this year, I received a peculiar message from the International Director of the English Chess Federation, Malcolm Pein, cryptically referring to events 'East of Ushuaia'. The contact in itself was a tad surprising because, in truth, I have not been in the best of relationships with Malcolm since he allied himself, during the FIDE Pres-idential Election last year, with a motley crew of tarnished individuals, on the Makropoulos ticket – many of whom he has subsequently disa-vowed. Still, he remains the most influential person, domestically, within English chess, and I am a FIDE Vice-President. Despite our previous differences, we are both pragmatic enough to understand that we are far more effective when working together harmoniously. When I finally spoke to him – inevi-tably after a Liverpool football match – he asked me whether I was involved with, or knew anything about, two chess tournaments and a match that had recently taken place in the British Overseas Territory of the Falkland Islands.

This was a perfectly legitimate question. Malcolm was well aware that, in 2016, I had been approached by Argentinian Grandmaster, Miguel Quinteros, with a view to holding a friendly match, over six boards, in the South Atlantic islands. I had liked the idea a lot. Money was in place, and, in fact, negotiations reached a fairly advanced stage, with discussions held, at Simpsons-in-the-Strand, in London, with a Falklands govern-ment representative. Regrettably though, the idea fell through when it failed to receive the green light from the capital, Port Stanley. Rightly or wrongly, they were afraid the match would be used for political purposes, as other sporting events have been in the past.

Sovereignty of the Falkland Islands has long been disputed. The first recorded landing on the uninhabited rocks was by British sailors in 1690.

A bit of history

Sovereignty of the islands has long been disputed. The first recorded landing on the uninhabited rocks was by British sailors in 1690. They named the channel which divides the two principal islands 'Falkland's Sound' in honour of the Treasurer of the Navy, Viscount Falkland. Over the following years, the European powers of Britain, France and Spain each established small settlements. In 1833, the somewhat ambiguous status of the islands was de facto, if not de jure, decided when Britain expelled an Argentine military garrison which had arrived there three months previously. Britain has maintained a continuous presence in the Falklands ever since. The long-established farming and fishing community, which now numbers around 3,200, is overwhelmingly of Anglo-Saxon stock.

The issue of sovereignty was largely quiescent during the rest of the 1800s, but began to resurface during the twentieth century, particularly under Peronism. Argentina claimed that the Falklands, or 'Malvinas' as they would have it, formed part of the province of Tierra del Fuego – rather ironically given that the southerly province itself did not become part of Argentina until decades after the Falklands was incorporated under the British Crown.

When falsehoods fester, the results can be deadly. The issue erupted upon the world stage when, on the 2nd April 1982, Argentina, under the military junta of General Galtieri, invaded the Falklands and triumphantly hoisted the blue and white flag. This unwelcome news took the government in London off guard, as they had only got wind of the operation when it was already underway and totally unstoppable.

The British Defence Minister, John Nott, gravely intoned the pessimistic official view of his department that the islands could not be retaken once seized. Unsurprisingly this meek and defeatist response did not mollify the Prime Minister, Margaret Thatcher. She instead sought the opinion of Sir Henry Leach – the Chief of the Naval

An impression from the 'Torneo de Ajedrez Islas del Sur' at the 'Lafont House', where the participants gathered after 9 p.m. after running the Falklands Marathon.

Staff – and it was his view that if a fleet of destroyers, frigates, landing craft, nuclear-powered submarines etc. were assembled, then victory could be achieved, despite the enormous logistical problems of operating thousands of kilometres from English shores.

It is not my intention to describe, in a chess magazine, the events of the subsequent weeks. Suffice it to say that the task force was duly despatched, and the Argentine invasion force, filled with unfortunate young conscripts, was routed in short order. 649 Argentine and 255 British soldiers died, along with 3 civilians. General Leopoldi Galtieri, along with his murderous death squads, were removed from power. Democracy in Argentina was thankfully restored.

The full pictures emerges

But returning, from this lengthy historical digression, to Malcolm Pein's original question, I had absolutely no idea about these tournaments. My initial reaction was to try

to turn the thing neatly into a public relations success. When the Argentinians, as I naively imagined, would politely ask the English Chess Federation for permission to rate these events, we should magnanimously agree, rather than taking nationalistic affront. It would show both our liberalism and their acknowledgement of our jurisdiction.

Alas, it soon became clear that this elegant solution was but a pipe-dream. The Argentinians had not the slightest intention of cooperating. Gradually, as information poured in, the full picture began to emerge. The match, between two ex-combatants, Coronel Mayor José Jimenez Corbalan and Lieutenant Marc Townsend, who had apparently fired at each other ineptly on the night of 8/9 June 1982, on the foothills of Mount Harriet, was (most conveniently) won 2½-1½ by the South American. One does not require a PhD in semiotics to understand this symbolically representing Argentina recapturing the Falklands.

The FIDE Qualification Commission, however, immediately rejected this submission because it is impossible to rate a match with no rated players. Bizarrely, though, it seems that no such provision exists in the FIDE regulations for *tournaments* without rated players. Therefore the '1er Abierto de Ajedrez Maraton de làs Islas', played in September (!!) 2018, and the 'Torneo de Ajedrez Islas del Sur' played in March 2019 were duly registered.

The arbiter was listed as Mario Petrucci, who is a member of the FIDE Executive Board. He holds the title of National Arbiter, which was awarded to him by the Argentine Federation, of which he is President. I would not dare to suggest impropriety, but it appears that the geographically-challenged Mr. Petrucci, far from being an experienced referee, has only ever arbitered tournaments in the Falklands, which he appears to believe is in Argentina.

Carrying live ammunition

The clandestine nature of the March tournament was symbolised by a two-kilometre walk through the darkness to the modest guest-house venue, 'Lafont House', where players would gather in the evening, after

One participant, Dr. Ujhelly, would later be fined £800 for attempting to carry live ammunition on the flight home.

9 p.m., after running the Falklands Marathon. One participant, Dr. Ujhelly, would later be fined £800 for attempting to carry live ammunition on the flight home. Subversive acts, such as unfurling the Argentinian flag at the Darwin Cemetery, were later proudly posted on *YouTube*, once the hitherto furtive operation had become public knowledge.

You don't have to be exceptionally cynical to contend that the otherwise incomprehensible omission of the words 'Falklands' or 'Malvinas' from the official report was done with the intentional aim of slipping these tournaments under the radar. The substitution of 'Puerto Argentino' – a term apparently used briefly during the 1982 invasion – for 'Port Stanley' was with the deliberate intention of duping FIDE into believing the tournament took place on Argentinian soil. 'Conjecture!' you might cry. Indeed, but the give-away is that no one but a moron or a madman would register tournaments for rating that

cannot be rated, without having an ulterior motive. That motive was spelled out literally in bold letters in a large article, replete with photographs, in the famous Argentine newspaper *Clarin* – 'The tournament was a way to exercise sovereignty'.

The Falkland Islands Legislative Assembly was incensed and wrote a letter of protest to FIDE. As it is not a chess body, it is not competent, for jurisdictional purposes, to submit such a complaint. The English Chess Federation most certainly is, however, and as the legacy body of the British Chess Federation (a founding member in 1924) it has responsibility for chess activity in all British Overseas Territories that are not members of FIDE. With almost unprecedented alacrity, the Presidents of both the Scottish and Welsh federations, who greatly value their independence, signed the letter as well.

People from all over the United Kingdom lost their lives in 1982 and no one forgets it. The British Foreign Secretary, Jeremy Hunt, tweeted his support: 'We are with the ECF on this. The Falkland Islands are part of the United Kingdom: the status of this particular square on the board is not in question!' That was not technically correct (being a British Overseas Territory it has a different legal status), but at least he was imprecisely right.

The Argentine Chess Federation was given several weeks by FIDE to state its case but, apart from the odd glib comment, chose not to do so. Eventually the FIDE Presidential Board, which moves at a glacial pace due to its inherited bloated structure, issued the following statement:

'FIDE has received a complaint that, between September 2018 and

At the first night of the new chess club that has sprung up in Stanley, the capital of the Falklands, nine members attended, including two Chileans and a veterinarian.

March 2019, two tournaments and a chess match, which took place in Stanley, in the British Overseas Territory of the Falkland Islands, were filed for consideration for FIDE rating by the Argentine Chess Federation.

'Federations reserve the exclusive right to submit tournaments for rating which take place in their territory.

'Because this was not done, and no attempt was made to seek permission or even inform the English Chess Federation, under whose purview chess in the Falkland Islands comes, the FIDE Qualification Commission will exclude these tournaments from rating.

'FIDE urges all federations to refrain from using chess tournaments for political purposes.'

Right to self-determination

With such high emotions, and national pride, it was of course too much to expect the matter to end there. The Argentine Embassy in Switzerland wrote a letter of complaint to FIDE (in French!) coincidentally, or not, just before the United Nations C24 meeting on decolonisation. It meets with the same legal objections as those of the Falkland Islands Legislative Assembly to FIDE. The

Nigel Short during a recent two-hour visit to Falkland Home in London, where he was received by representative Matthew Ware.

United Nations supports the right to self-determination. In the 2013 referendum the Falkland islanders voted 99.8% for the continuation of its status as a British Overseas Territory. Quod erat demonstrandum.

As Margaret Thatcher said: 'We were defending our honour as a nation, and principles of fundamental importance to the whole world – above all, that aggressors should never succeed, and that international law should prevail...' As the great Argentinian writer, Jorge Luis Borges, said of the Falklands War, that it was 'a fight between two bald men over a comb'. I don't know whether such divergent views are reconcilable, but I somehow feel that both were simultaneously right.

On the positive side, with all the publicity, a new chess club has sprung up in Stanley, organised by the writer Rita Seagull. The first night, at the amusingly-named Malvina House Hotel, was attended by nine members, including two Chileans and a veterinarian, whom I once played in a simul in the UK. The following week attracted three new enthusiasts. Let us hope the expansion continues.

This may all seem very dim and distant to most people and probably it is. But remember that next time you are sitting in a Greek taverna, by the Mediterranean, eating (frozen) calamari, there is a 60% chance that the food on your plate has come from the Falklands. ∎

Alexander Grischuk and Ian Nepomniachtchi battle it out in the final of the Moscow Grand Prix. The ornamental ceiling betrays that this is the Great Hall of the Central Chess Club.

FIDE Grand Prix series sets off in Moscow

Nepomniachtchi triumphs on home turf

On the inside the Central Chess Club on Gogol Boulevard was barely recognizable as its walls were draped in the black and white of World Chess, but that did not stop the Russian participants from calling the shots. In the final of the Moscow Grand Prix **VLADIMIR BARSKY** saw Ian Nepomniachtchi get the better of Alexander Grischuk as both his countrymen collected precious GP points.

NIKI RIGA

The Moscow stage of the FIDE Grand Prix took place in the famous Central Chess Club. A place that, so to speak, is 'sacred'. All the World Champions from Botvinnik to Carlsen have played here. The fifth champion Max Euwe also visited this building many times, when he came to Moscow in the capacity of FIDE President.

Recently this old residence underwent a major restoration, and it looks radiant. The splendid Great Hall, where balls were once held, and where the famous singer Feodor Chaliapin and the composer Sergei Rachmaninoff performed... We watched with sadness as a whole truck-load of black décor was brought to Gogol Boulevard, and the hall was draped from floor to ceiling, even blocking the windows.

Gradually we became accustomed to the gloomy World Chess style. When events are held in buildings that obviously need redecoration, black draping is a good solution. But why here? After the end of the tournament I asked Ian Nepomniachtchi whether he liked the appearance of the hall. Winners are usually satisfied with everything, but Ian replied: 'Initially it was difficult – for 16 participants, the hall in this form was cramped. The décor takes a lot of space, and room also has to be left for the spectators. And you can't see what is happening on the boulevard. Sasha Grischuk told me practically the same thing: during the Russian Championship you could look out of the window – snow was falling, and you could meditate... Such gentle nostalgia. I would not say that I am delighted with this design, since the hall is itself very beautiful. I think that the organizers could have made an exception and changed their style for the duration of this tournament.'

A real centre piece

The pairings were made a couple of hours before the start, so that no one was able to make meaningful preparations for their opponent. Possibly thanks to this the first round turned out to an exceptionally fighting one.

The real centre-piece was the duel between top-seed Anish Giri and Daniil Dubov. The current World Rapid Champion is famed for his original opening ideas and his readiness to give up a pawn or even two for the initiative. Anish accepted the

challenge, but found himself on unfamiliar territory. In the first game he managed to defend, but not in the second. 'I will have to draw some serious conclusions from this match, and not only chess conclusions', Anish philosophically remarked after the end of the encounter.

Here is that spectacular game with notes by the winner.

NOTES BY
Daniil Dubov

Daniil Dubov
Anish Giri
Moscow 2019 (1.2)
Slav Defence, Botvinnik Variation

1.d4 ♘f6 2.c4 e6 3.♘f3 d5 4.♗g5!?

Chess is actually quite a difficult game. I have played a lot of games with 4.♗g5 here, but after a short training session with a very smart guy (I'll reveal his name and give him all the credit after the whole Grand Prix

The splendid Great Hall, where balls were once held, and where the famous singer Feodor Chaliapin and the composer Sergei Rachmaninoff performed...

FIDE Grand Prix

The FIDE Grand Prix consists of four tournaments, which will be held this year in Moscow, Riga, Hamburg and Tel Aviv. Taking part in the series are 22 grandmasters, each of whom will have three attempts. The tournaments are held on a knock-out system with 16 participants. The prize fund for one tournament is 130,000 euros, and for the entire series – 800,000 euros. The winner of a stage receives 8 points, the other finalist 5, the semi-finalists 3 each, and the quarter-finalists 1 each. Every match won without a tie-break is awarded an additional point.

Moscow 2019 FIDE GP

First round	
Grischuk-Karjakin	1½-½
Svidler-Vitiugov	1½-½
Giri-**Dubov**	½-1½
Radjabov-**Nakamura**	1½-2½
Duda-**So**	1½-2½
Nepomniachtchi-Aronian	1½-½
Wei Yi-**Jakovenko**	½-1½
Wojtaszek-Mamedyarov	1½-½

Quarter Final	
Nakamura-Dubov	2½-1½
Grischuk-So	2½-1½
Wei Yi-**Nepomniachtchi**	1½-2½
Svidler-**Wojtaszek**	½-1½

Semi-Final	
Grischuk-Nakamura	1½-½
Nepomniachtchi-Wojtaszek	3½-2½

Final	
Nepomniachtchi-Grischuk	2½-½

FIDE GP – standings

1	Ian Nepomniachtchi	8 + 1 = 9
2	Alexander Grischuk	5 + 2 = 7
3	Radoslaw Wojtaszek	3 + 2 = 5
4	Hikaru Nakamura	3 + 0 = 3
5	Peter Svidler	1 + 1 = 2
6	Wei Yi	1 + 1 = 2
7	Daniil Dubov	1 + 1 = 2
8	Wesley So	1 + 0 = 1

series has come to an end) a few weeks before the start of the Moscow GP, I realized that I didn't have a single idea about what I was doing. We (he) managed to find some new ideas and upgrade my knowledge quite a bit.

4...dxc4!?
Obviously not the only move, but the most ambitious one. As far as I know it's considered to be some kind of an official refutation, but that view will probably change quite soon.
5.e4! That was one of our main points. I've tried some stupid 5.♕a4+ and other moves, but 5.e4 is by far the most challenging move.
5...b5 6.a4 c6 7.♘c3

Now we have transposed to the Botvinnik Variation where White has played 7.a4 instead of the main line with 7.e5, but this doesn't make it any worse for White.
7...b4 Black has a lot of alternatives, but I'm not going to publish the results of our work. Anish's choice is not a real mistake yet, but the edge is getting closer.
8.♘b1 ♗a6 9.e5!? 9.♕c1!? is also reasonable, if White wants to slow down a bit.
9...h6

10.♗xf6
During the game I actually couldn't believe that 10.♗h4 g5 11.exf6 gxh4 12.♘bd2 is better for Black than the position in the game. Come on, it's all about development and Black has only given a stupid pawn for the tempi? Still, I decided that it makes sense to follow the lines I'd checked precisely. The explanation is probably that pawns can also matter sometimes.

10...gxf6 11.exf6 c5
First I was slightly worried about 11...♕d5, but then I realized that 12.♕c2! is the move and I'm in time to capture c4 (12.♘bd2? c3 is the point): 12...b3 13.♕c3 c5 14.♘bd2 with an edge for White.
12.♘bd2

12...c3?!
The first mistake of the game. I knew that 12...♘c6! is the move and it's OK for Black, but he is down to only moves in most of the lines that follow: 13.♗xc4 ♗xc4 14.♘xc4 ♕xf6.

ANALYSIS DIAGRAM

And now White has different attempts, but Black is holding: 15.♕e2 (15.a5!?; 15.dxc5 ♖d8) 15...♘xd4

16.♘xd4 cxd4! 17.♘e5 (or 17.♘b6 axb6 18.♕b5+ ♔e7 19.♕xb4+ ♔d7 20.♕b5+ ♔c7 21.♖c1+ ♗c5 22.♖xc5+ bxc5 23.♕xc5+ with a draw) 17...d3 18.♕e4 ♖c8 19.♘xd3 ♗d6, with equality.

13.bxc3 bxc3 14.♘e4 cxd4

15.♗b5+!

My general approach for this crazy kind of positions is quite simple: as I know I'm not capable of calculating everything, I'm trying to play the move I like during the first seconds of thought. Getting a pawn to b5 and restricting the black knight felt extremely natural.

15...♗xb5 16.axb5

16...♕d5?

Now White is winning. 16...d3! was the only move. I don't know if White is winning here, but at least I failed to prove it with an engine. Which doesn't mean Black is holding, as

Daniil Dubov seems to agree that in summer the tree-lined promenade in front of the Central Chess Club is a perfect place for an outdoor simul.

it's a common mistake to think you can never go wrong following the engine's lines. It feels extremely close and I won't be surprised if somebody will find a win for White.

Here are some sample lines that I found:

– 17.0-0 c2! 18.♕d2 ♕d5! 19.♘c3 ♕d6! 20.b6 ♘d7 21.b7 ♖b8 and Black is holding, although he's always down to only moves: 22.♘b5 ♕c6 23.♕xd3 ♕xb7 24.♘bd4 ♖c8 25.♖fc1 ♘f6 26.♖xc2 ♖xc2 27.♕xc2 ♗b4 28.♕a4+ ♔f8 29.♖b1 a5 30.♕xa5 ♗xa5 31.♖xb7 ♔g8, with equality.

– The simple way is 17.♘xc3 ♘d7 18.0-0 ♘xf6 19.♘e5 ♗g7 20.♘c6 ♕d6 21.♕f3 0-0 22.♖fd1 with an edge for White.

17.♕xd4 Not that I had a choice...

17...♕xb5

... but neither did he.

18.♘xc3?

I decided to play what felt most natural to me again, planning 0-0-0, but missed a win. Not a very big sensation in this kind of position, plus I was extremely tempted by the idea of playing 0-0-0...

But after 18.♘e5! White is winning: 18...♘d7 (if 18...♕b4!? then 19.♖a4! ♕xd4 20.♖xd4 and White is winning, which wasn't obvious at all during the game. If you think it's quite simple because Black doesn't have good pieces at all – don't worry, you will be given an example of pretty the same position where Black is completely fine quite soon) 19.♖a5! (this is the main point) 19...♕b1+

As I know I'm not capable of calculating everything, I'm trying to play the move I like during the first seconds of thought.

20.♔e2 ♕b2+ 21.♔f3 ♘xe5+
22.♕xe5 ♖c8 23.♖c1!

ANALYSIS DIAGRAM

and White is winning. Here it's kind of easier, as the white king is almost safe, which means Black will be mated soon. Not that I really missed the whole idea of 19.♖a5, but it's fair to say that I wanted to play 18.♘xc3 and I was mostly trying to make it work.

18...♗b4

19.0-0-0!

The exclamation mark is mostly given for the whole idea, but White didn't exactly have a real alternative here.

After 19.♘d2 ♗xc3 20.♕xc3 ♘c6 Black is fine.

19...♕a5?!

The most natural move, but not the best one.

Not that I missed 19...♕b6!, but I just couldn't get when those endgames are really dangerous for Black and when they are not. I also wasn't sure at all that I'm better, so I was mostly concentrated on making sure I'm not losing by force. Play then could continue: 20.♔c2 (on 20.♘b5, 20...♕c6+ is the only move, but after 21.♔b1 ♘a6 Black takes over) 20...♕xd4 21.♖xd4 ♗xc3 22.♔xc3 ♘d7 23.♖a1 ♘xf6 24.♖da4 and it will be a draw.

20.♘b5!

I kept following my strategy. I felt like the combination of ♘b5/♔b1 looked extremely nice. It's becoming almost study-like, so once I realized that this was not a blunder I played it.

But also interesting was 20.♖d3!? ♕b6 21.♕c4 ♘a6 22.♔d1.

20...♘a6 21.♕d7+ ♔f8 22.♔b1!

As said, this was my main point. Normally, with such a king you need desperately to mate first, as otherwise you will be mated yourself. The position from the game is quite an unusual example of trying to play positional chess in a crazy position with both kings weakened. My basic point is quite simple: there's no way for the black rooks to join the game, so I need to protect my king first and then I'll bring all the pieces and win. Black should always watch back-rank

mating threats, so I have a chance.

22...♗a3?

By far the most natural move again. But not the best. Here 22...♗c5!

ANALYSIS DIAGRAM

seems to hold, but it's obviously extremely dangerous for Black and he's always down to dozens of only moves. So, Black plays exactly only moves in all the following lines: 23.♘e5 ♕b4+ 24.♔c2 ♕a4+ 25.♔d3 ♖h7 26.♔e2 ♕e4+ 27.♔f1 ♗b6 and Black is holding.

23.♖d2!? ♔g8 24.♖hd1 ♖b8 25.♖b2 ♕a4! 26.♖d3 ♕f4 27.♖d2 (or 27.♘fd4 ♗xd4 28.♕xd4 ♕xd4 29.♖g3+ ♔f8 30.♘xd4 ♖xb2+ 31.♔xb2 ♘c5 32.♖a3 ♘d7 33.♖xa7 ♘xf6, with a draw) 27...♖xf6 28.♘e4 ♕e5 29.♘bc3 ♖xb2+ 30.♔xb2 ♕b8+! 31.♔a1 ♗a3! 32.♘b5 ♕e5+! 33.♘d4 ♗f8! 34.♖f3 ♖h7 35.♘f6+ ♔h8 36.♘xh7 ♕a5+, and a draw, as the white king cannot escape the checks.

23.♖d3! While Anish was thinking, I realized that Black was completely lost unless I'm blundering something simple. The king goes back to the kingside and finally gets to safety, which means the game is over.

23...♕b4+

On 23...♖b8 White plays 24.♖b3! (Black's point is 24.♘fd4 ♕c7! and he has saved himself, which I mentioned after the game) 24...♕a4 25.♘d2 and White wins.

24.♔c2 ♕a4+

Or 24...♕b2+ 25.♔d1 ♕c1+ 26.♔e2 ♕xh1 27.♕d8+ ♖xd8 28.♖xd8 mate.

25.♔d2 ♗b4+ 26.♔e2 ♔g8

Not the most trivial +6 position that I've seen. Now basically more or less everything wins, I just need to avoid blunders and prevent the rook on h8 from getting out.

27.♘e5 ♕c2+ 28.♔f3 ♖f8 29.♖hd1

A good alternative was 29.♖a1!? ♘c5 30.♕d4 h5 31.♕e3 ♖h7 32.♖c1, and White wins.

29...h5!

Black goes for his last chance. I had completely missed the idea of ...h5 followed by ...♖h6. Fortunately, White has a way (the only way!) to prevent it.

30.♕d4! ♖h7

After 30...♗c5, 31.♕h4! is the only move. Originally I had missed the fact that I have this weird square on h4 to protect f2.

31.♕f4

They normally say 'the rest is simple' in a stable +10 position. Well, chesswise it was.

31...♗c5 32.♘d4 ♕a2 33.♖1d2 ♕d5+ 34.♔e2

(Lap number 4?)

34...♗b4 35.♘dc6 ♕c5

35...♖xd2 runs into 36.♕g3+.

36.♘e7+ ♔h8

And Anish resigned, which prevented me from playing 37.♘xf7+, with a simple mate.

I like this game mostly because it shows how sharp and complex chess can be. You can try to analyse it by yourself, then check some random chessbomb notes, then you come home and check it briefly with your

I like this game mostly because it shows how sharp and complex chess can be.

laptop and then you finally get time to check it precisely with a very strong engine for a few hours. Believe me, all the conclusions will differ and probably the last one won't be the end of the story.

■ ■ ■

Not so harmless

Ian Nepomniachtchi confidently outplayed Levon Aronian 1½-½. The winner had this to say: 'I did a lot of preparation with Volodya Potkin, and we worked well. A couple of times I was able to surprise my opponents, even with Black. Against Aronian we unearthed an old variation, which, surprisingly enough, 'fired'. It was also tested in some FIDE Grand Prix tournaments, but 10 years ago: in 2009 it was played by Kamsky and Ivanchuk. As it turned out, the variation is not so harmless.'

NOTES BY
Ian Nepomniachtchi

Ian Nepomniachtchi
Levon Aronian
Moscow 2019 (1.1)
Ruy Lopez, Anti-Marshall Variation

1.e4 e5 2.♘f3 ♘c6 3.♗b5 a6 4.♗a4 ♘f6 5.0-0 ♗e7 6.♖e1 b5 7.♗b3 0-0 8.d4

It is surprising, but against my opponent, the main proponent of the Marshall Attack these days, this move has been rather rarely employed.

8...♘xd4

9.♗xf7+!? 9.♘xd4 exd4 10.e5 ♘e8 11.c3 is more popular, as played by Harikrishna against Aronian last year.

9...♖xf7 10.♘xe5 ♖f8

Any attempts to obtain two pieces for a rook are unsuccessful: 10...♘e6 11.♘xf7 ♔xf7 12.e5; 10...♘c6 11.♘xf7 ♔xf7 12.e5; 10...c5 11.♘xf7 ♔xf7 12.e5.

11.♕xd4

This rather neglected variation has occurred at least three times in the games of Peter Leko. As soon as it became clear that even such a metic-

ulous theoretician experienced some problems in equalizing here, in my eyes the reputation of the entire system grew greatly.

11...♗b7

Black also has another available plan: 11...c5 12.♕d1 ♕c7 13.♘g4 ♘xg4 14.♕xg4 d5 15.♕h5 dxe4 16.♕d5+ ♔h8 17.♕xa8 ♗b7 18.♕a7 ♖a8 19.♗f4!? ♕c6 20.♕xa8+ ♗xa8 21.♗e3

ANALYSIS DIAGRAM

and the two rooks proved stronger than the queen, Ivanchuk-Leko, 2008.

12.♘c3 c5 13.♕d1 b4

This move leads to more forcing play than 13...♕c7 or 13...♕e8. It must be said that nearly everywhere Black has decent compensation for the pawn.

14.♘d5 ♘xd5 15.exd5 ♗d6

16.c4

Here White has mainly played 16.f4, after which it is not easy to avoid simplification: 16...♗xe5 17.fxe5 ♕h4 18.♗e3 ♕c4 19.b3 ♕xd5 20.♕xd5+ ♗xd5 21.♖ed1 ♗e6 22.♗xc5 ♖fc8 23.♗xb4 ♖xc2, and soon the players agreed a draw, Amin-Leko, 2011.

16...bxc3 Here for the first time Levon had a long think. It is hard to

say what induced the choice of this particular moment, since there is no alternative to the *en passant* capture. For example, 16...♗xe5 17.♖xe5 ♖xf2 (17...♕f6 18.♕e1) 18.♗g5 ♕f8 19.♕g4, and things are bad for Black.
17.bxc3

17...a5?
This multi-purpose move is not in accordance with the rhythm of the position. Yes, the bishop (or the rook) acquires the convenient a6-square, but Black cannot delay: the white pieces are about to emerge and the compensation for the pawn will evaporate.
17...♕f6 was critical. After the game Levon said that he did not like 18.♘g4 ♕xc3 19.♖b1 ♖ab8 20.♖b6, with a crushing initiative for White. But instead of the capture on c3 the quiet move 18...♕f5 gives Black excellent counterplay.
18.♘f3!? 18.f4 was possibly stronger, but I reasoned that Black was effectively losing a move in the 17...♕f6 18.♘f3 variation.
18...♕f6 The most logical move, as 19.c4 was threatened.
19.♗g5 White does not cling on to the material, preferring activity.

19...♕g6 As *The Iliad* teaches, accepting Greek gifts is dangerous: after 19...♕xc3 20.♖b1 ♗a6 21.♖b3 ♕c4 22.♗e7 ♗xe7 23.♖xe7 the white pieces break in to Troy.
20.♗e7 The predatory glances of the black bishops, aimed at the kingside, considerably unnerved me, and therefore I considered the exchange of one of them to be an urgent matter.
20...♗xe7 21.♖xe7 ♕d6
The white pawns are easy targets, but capturing them proves to be fraught with danger.
Possibly Black should have fought for the e-file: 21...♖ae8 22.♖xe8 ♖xe8 23.c4 d6 24.♘d2 ♗c8 25.♘f1 ♗f5, with partial compensation.

22.♕e2
The artificial 22.♕e1?, so that in certain variations the queen should not come under attack, would have led to a change of scene: 22...♖xf3! 23.gxf3 ♕g6+ 24.♔h1 ♗xd5, and White has to concern himself with saving the game.
22...♗xd5
22...♖xf3? does not work now: 23.gxf3 ♕g6+ 24.♔h1 ♗xd5 25.♖g1, and wins.
23.♖d1

23...♖ab8
23...♗xf3?! 24.♕c4+ (the endgame after 24.♖xd6 ♗xe2 25.♖xe2 ♖a7 is rather unpleasant, but by no means

Nepomniachtchi-Aronian: 'A third time he cast his net, and what he found in his net was a fish – no ordinary fish, but a golden fish.'

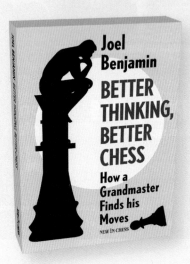
hopeless for Black) 24...♗d5 25.♖xd5 ♕xe7 26.♖xd7+ ♕f7 27.♖xf7 ♖xf7 28.a4!, and the white queen acquires good prospects of eating up the weak enemy pawns.

24.♘e1?!
After 24.h3 ♗xf3 25.♕c4+ ♗d5 26.♕xd5+ (26.♖xd5 ♖b1+! 27.♖d1+ ♔h8, and the worst for Black is over) 26...♖xd5 27.♖xd5 ♖f7 28.♖e2 White emerges with a solid advantage in the rook ending, but before the opponent's impending time-trouble I did not want to allow simplification.
24.♖e5 ♗xf3 25.♕c4+ ♗d5 26.♖exd5 ♕e6 leads to similar positions: the advantage may prove insufficient, with the game reducing to a well-known drawn position '3 against 2'.
24...♕c6 The only move.
25.♕e5 ♗f7

It transpires that the timid-looking bishop has taken aim at the a2-pawn. Unprecedented dexterity is demanded of White, to avoid completely squandering his advantage.
26.♖dxd7
Nothing is promised by 26.♖d6 ♕c7, when Black is close to equality.

26...♖fe8 27.♕f4 Better was 27.♕f5 ♖xe7 (27...♕f6 28.♕xc5) 28.♖xe7 ♕d5 29.♕f4 ♕b7 30.♖e2, with a slight advantage for White.
27...♕f6 28.♖xe8+ ♖xe8 29.♕d2

29...♕e6? The exchange of rooks in this version is a serious mistake. After 29...♕b6 30.h3 ♕b1 31.♖d8 h6 Black is alright, but 29...♕f4! 30.♘f3 ♕xd2 31.♖xd2 a4 32.a3 ♗h5 was even more accurate, with equality.
30.♖d8 h6 31.♖xe8+ ♕xe8 32.a3

White is a sound pawn to the good, and in time the knight will find an optimal post. In addition, Black's problems were aggravated by time-trouble.
32...♕a4 33.♕c1 ♗g6 34.♘f3 ♕b3 35.♘e5 ♗c2 36.♘g4

Now the c3-pawn is indirectly defended.

36...a4 36...♕xc3?? 37.♘e3. **37.h3 ♗f5 38.♘e5 ♔h7 39.♔h2 ♕a2 40.♔g1 ♔g8** The time-control was reached. Levon managed to make this move literally a second before 'the fall of his flag', and therefore there is no great point in drawing attention to the quality of the two sides' play.

41.♕f4 41.c4 was also thematic, but I wanted to find out whether my opponent would sacrifice a piece and make it easier for White to convert his advantage. O sancta simplicitas!

41...♕xa3

In the event of 41...♗c2 42.♕c4+ ♕xc4 43.♘xc4 ♔f7 44.f4 ♗b3 45.♘d2 Black's fate is also unenviable.

42.♕xf5 ♕xc3 42...♕b3 43.♘d3 a3 44.♘xc5 ♕d1+ 45.♔h2 a2 46.♕e6+ ♔h7 47.♕xa2 ♕d6+ 48.g3 ♕xc5 49.♕c2+ would not have helped to maintain the intrigue.

43.♘c6?

'One day he cast his net, And all he caught in his net was mud.' (Lines from Alexander Pushkin's *A Tale about a Fisherman and a Fish* – translator.)

'One day he cast his net, And all he caught in his net was mud.'

Mate, as is well known, ends the game! It was annoying that I almost immediately found the attractive idea 43.♕e6+ ♔h8 44.♘g6+ ♔h7 45.♕e8 a3 46.h4! a2 47.h5 a1♕+ 48.♔h2, but, as it is said, I did not believe my luck. **43...♔h8 44.♕f7 ♕b3 45.♕e8+ ♔h7 46.♕e4+ ♔h8 47.♘a5**

As a result of intricate manoeuvres White nevertheless stops the pawns. **47...♕d1+ 48.♔h2 ♕d6+ 49.f4 a3**

Or 49...♕d4 50.♕xd4 cxd4 51.♔g3 a3 52.♘b3 and wins.

50.♕a4?

'He cast his net a second time, And all he caught in his net was weed.'

In the sixth hour of play, alas, it proved not so easy to find 50.♘c4! ♕a6 51.♘e5! a2 52.♘f7+ ♔g8 53.♕e8+ ♔h7 54.f5. However, the

desire to eliminate the dangerous pawns is fully understandable.

50...c4

Black also fails to save the game with 50...♕d3 51.♕b3 c4 52.♕a2 h5 53.♘xc4 h4 54.♕xa3 ♕xc4 55.♕f8+ ♔h7 56.♕f5+ ♔g8 57.♕g5.

51.♕xc4 ♕d2

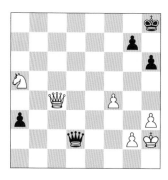

52.♘b3

Having halted, by hook or by crook, the nimble black pawns, White forgot that it was possible simply to capture them! The draughts-like combination 52.♕c8+ ♔h7 53.♕f5+ ♔g8 (53...♔h8 54.♕f8+ ♔h7 55.♕xa3 and wins) 54.♘c4 ♕b4 55.♕d5+ ♔h7 56.♕d3+ ♔h8 57.♘xa3 could have concluded this error-strewn game.

52...♕e3 53.♘c1 h5

Of course, here Black has no real saving chances, but a psychic attack is a fearsome weapon.

54.h4?!

54.♘e2 h4 55.♘g1 – the knight, so to speak, goes 'back to the drawing-board' and heads for g5.

54...♕e7 55.♕c8+ ♔h7 56.♕f5+ g6 57.♕h3 ♕f7

Here things had become serious.

First, a queen endgame with two extra pawns on the h- and g-files is a 'table-base' draw (however, for a human practically unattainable). Second, such a stream of mistakes and oversights rarely goes unpunished.

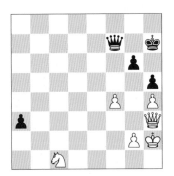

58.f5?

58.♕e3 a2 59.♘xa2 ♕xa2 60.♕e7+ ♔g8 61.f5 gxf5 62.♕g5+ leads to the afore-mentioned ending.

58.♕xa3 ♕xf4+ 59.♔g1 ♕d4+ 60.♔f1 ♕f4+ 61.♔e2 ♕e4+ 62.♔d1 ♕xh4 63.♕f3 should win without any great problems.

But the move in the game, to all appearances, throws away the win.

58...♕c7+ 59.♔g3 ♕xc1 60.♕xg6+ ♔h8 61.♕xh5+ ♔g7 62.♕g6+ ♔f8 63.♕f6+ ♔e8?

The wrong way!

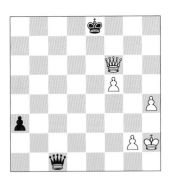

64.♕e6+?

64.♕e5+! ♔f7 65.f6 ♕h6 66.♕e7+ ♔g6 67.f7 ♕f4+ 68.♔h3 ♕f5+ 69.♔g3 ♕xf7 70.♕xa3 would have been back to square one.

64...♔f8 65.♕d6+ ♔f7 66.♕e6+ ♔f8 67.♕f6+ ♔g8!

Levon did not have to be cajoled a second time, and he chooses the lesser of the two evils.

68.♕e5

68...♔f7?

68...♕h6! looks counter-intuitive: one doesn't want to abandon the a3-pawn to its fate, but this is the move that forces a draw. Here is one of the main variations: 69.♕g3+ ♔f7□ 70.♕b3+ ♔e8 71.♕xa3 ♕xh4+ 72.♕h3 ♕f4+ 73.♔g1 ♕c1+ 74.♔f2 ♕d2+ 75.♔g3 ♕e3+ 76.♔g4 ♕d4+, and Black saves himself.

69.f6

'A third time he cast his net, and what he found in his net was a fish – no ordinary fish, but a golden fish.'

69...♕c4 69...♕h6 70.♕e7+ ♔g6 71.f7 ♕f4+ 72.♔h3 ♕f5+ 73.♔g3 ♕xf7 74.♕xa3 etc. was comparatively the best chance.

70.♕e7+ ♔g6 71.♕g7+ ♔f5 72.♕g5+

Black resigned. With his king cut off on the opposite wing there is no sense in resisting: 72...♔e4 73.♕g4+ ♔d5 74.♕xc4+ ♔xc4 75.f7 a2 76.f8♕ a1♕ 77.♕f4+, with an easy win.

A very nervy game, conveying the atmosphere of a knock-out tournament.

■ ■ ■

The Mamedyarov-Wojtaszek match took a dramatic course. In the first game Shakh gained a serious advantage with Black, and many spectators had already mentally chalked up a point for him. At some point my colleagues and I went out onto the boulevard and bumped into a tense and serious Alina Kashlinskaya, who was hurrying to the club. 'When are you leaving Moscow?', one of us not very tactfully enquired. 'We are not in a rush!', Alina promptly exclaimed. 'We are hoping to stay to the end of the Grand Prix!'. Perhaps her confidence was telepathically transmitted to Radek, her husband, as on the board miracles began to occur.

Radoslaw Wojtaszek
Shakhriyar Mamedyarov
Moscow 2019 (1.1)

position after 54.♖a5

54...♗b7

An attempt to win 'with every comfort'. But Black should have slightly exerted himself: after 54...♘c6! 55.♖xa6 ♖b7 56.♖f8 (the pawn cannot be saved: 56.♖a4 ♗b3) 56...♘e5 57.♖a4 ♘xb4 he will soon be able to get at the key g4-pawn.

55.♖a3 ♔d5?

This position should find its way into endgame books as a striking example of an exception to a rule: centralization is not a panacea! Remember how Tarrasch joked: 'A rook should always be placed behind a passed pawn, with the exception of those cases when this is bad!' After the accurate 55...♔c7 56.♖f8 ♖d6 Black retains winning chances.

56.♖c3! The centralized king has fallen into a rook 'pincer'! The sharp change of scene had a discouraging effect on Mamedyarov.

56...♗c6?? He should have reconciled himself to a repetition of moves: 56...♘b5 57.♖d3+ ♘d4 58.♖c3 (in the event of 58.♔e3 ♔c4 59.♖d2 ♗c6 only White is taking a risk).

57.♔e3! ♘b3 A check on c5, winning the knight, was threatened, and after 57...♘b5 58.♖c5+ ♔d6 59.♖e6+ the bishop is lost.
58.♖e6! ♗b5 **59.♖xb3** ♔c4 **60.♖b1** ♔c3 **61.♖xf6**
And White won.

This gift of fate inspired Wojtaszek: he easily made a draw in the return game, in the quarter final he defeated Svidler, and he was close to knocking out Nepomniachtchi, but Ian enjoyed an enormous slice of luck.

Mention should be made of Grischuk's hard-earned win over Karjakin: in the second game Sasha demonstrated excellent endgame technique, converting a minimal advantage against the grandmaster who has been nicknamed the 'Minister of Defence'.

Hikaru Nakamura, one of the favourites and a favourite subject for selfies, was eliminated in the semi-finals.

Russia vs the World

The quarter final was transformed into a 'Russia-World' match, ending in a 2-2 draw.

Only Wojtaszek won in normal time, after refuting Svidler's risky play in the second game. Nakamura showed that he is rightly considered one of the best in play with a shortened time control. Grischuk called him the No. 2 after Carlsen, and such a compliment is worth a great deal!

Daniil Dubov
Hikaru Nakamura
Moscow 2019 (2.3)

position after 32...♔f7

The position is roughly equal, but to his misfortune White decided to treat himself to the central pawn: **33.♖d8?**

♗e7 **34.♖xd5** ♗c8! Elegant! Because of the weakness of the long diagonal the knight cannot move from c5 (35.♘d3 ♖b1+ 36. ♔h2 ♗b7). With his next move Black will pin it, and then begin pursuing the rook.
35.♔f1 ♖b5! **36.♔e2** ♗e6
37.♘xe6 ♖xd5 **38.♘c5 f5**

And Black converted his exchange advantage.

In the first additional game Nepomniachtchi was close to losing – he had to save himself a piece down. Although he recently had a similar situation in a game with a classical time control at the World Team Championship in Astana – and, no problem, he coped. And in the return game Ian trapped the black queen.

Ian Nepomniachtchi
Wei Yi
Moscow 2019 (2.4)

position after 20.♖e2

The Chinese grandmaster had already played a hybrid of the Caro-Kann and the Pirc Defence that was seen in this game, and Ian was excellently prepared, employing a strong novelty on the 17th move. Black needed to be patient, but he wanted to get rid of the powerful knight on e5. **20...f6? 21.h4! ♕f5 22.♗c2** The queen has no more moves, and it had to be given up: **22...♕xc2 23.♖xc2 fxe5 24.dxe5 ♗g4 25.♕d3 ♗f5 26.♕d1 ♗xc2 27.♕xc2**

Ian did not miss his chance and he earned his passage to the semi-final.

The last to reach the semi-finals was Grischuk. With Black, in reply to 1.e4 he pinned his hopes on the Sveshnikov Variation, to which Wesley So was unable to find the key. In the classical game Black easily defended, and in the rapid he altogether gained the initiative. According to Grischuk, he considered a draw in this game to be the normal outcome, but in the

interval between games he went onto one of the sites and discovered that he had been called a 'chicken': that is to say, in the final position he had been afraid to play for a win. And indeed, the computer promises Black a big advantage – one and a half pawns.

It would appear that the teasing provoked Grischuk, and he conducted the second game very powerfully. After gaining a stable advantage from the opening, he accurately converted this into a win. Grischuk assessed his endgame technique as '50% Magnus', but he was clearly being modest.

Another highlight

In the semi-final one of the most attractive games of the tournament was played.

NOTES BY
Alexander Grischuk

Alexander Grischuk
Hikaru Nakamura
Moscow 2019 (3.2)
Catalan Opening, Open Variation

'I think I can safely say that nobody understands quantum mechanics.'
Richard Feynman,
Nobel Prize-winner in Physics

To be honest, rather a long time ago I became tired of annotating my games, but this one turned out to be genuinely good and important from the competitive point of view. A good moment to make an exception.
1.d4 ♘f6 2.c4 e6 3.♘f3 d5 4.g3 ♗e7 5.♗g2 0-0 6.0-0 dxc4

7.♕c2 b5

Hikaru had already played this five or six times, so that it did not come as a surprise to me, although, in my view, the variation is rather dubious.
8.a4 b4 9.♘fd2 c6 10.♘xc4 ♕xd4 11.♖d1 ♕c5 12.♗e3 ♕h5 13.♘bd2 ♘g4 14.♘f3 ♘xe3 15.♘xe3 a5 To the untrained eye the series of moves beginning with 8.a4 looks rather strange, but in fact all this is quite forced, at least on Black's part.
16.♘d4

If desired, this position can be analysed for days on end, because the computer gives 'conflicting evidence' even after many hours of consideration, but to me it seems quite obvious that the initiative is on White's side, from both the analytical and the practical point of view.
16...♗a6 17.♖ac1 ♖c8 18.♗f3

Alexander Grischuk assessed his endgame technique as '50% Magnus', but he was clearly being modest.

18...♕g6

The following variation is very important: 18...♕e5 19.♘g4! ♕c7 20.♕b3! ♖a7!.

ANALYSIS DIAGRAM

Now nothing is given by the immediate 21.♘xc6 ♘xc6 22.♖xc6 ♕b8 23.♕e3 ♖xc6 24.♗xc6 ♖c7 25.♘e5 h6, when Black is alright.
21.♗e4!! is correct. Now 22.♘xe6 is threatened, therefore 21...♗f8 is more or less forced, and only now 22.♘xc6 ♘xc6 23.♖xc6, when after 23...♕b8 24.♕e3 ♖xc6 25.♗xc6 ♖c7 26.♘e5 White has a big advantage. Why is it so important that the bishop is on f8, and not on e7? I don't know. Some kind of chess quantum mechanics.
19.♗e4 ♕h5 20.♗f3 ♕g6 21.♗e4 ♕h5

It isn't often that Alexander Grischuk plays a game that lives up to his own high standards, so don't miss his comments.

22.♔g2 Now, when the black queen has become stuck on the kingside, it looks logical to try and cramp it even more; hence this and the two following moves.
22...♖a7 23.h4 g6 If Black tries to manage without this move, then at some point after g3-g4 he may lose his queen.
24.f4 ♕h6

25.♘b3? Of course, I very much didn't want to make this frankly mediocre move. For about half an hour I tried to find an advantage after 25.♘g4 ♕g7 26.♘e5 ♖ac7 27.♗f3 ♗f6 (the computer attempts to hang on with 27...♕f8 28.h5 gxh5 29.♗xh5

♗f6, but this bears little relation to a practical game) 28.♕c5 ♗xe5 29.fxe5 ♘d7 30.♕xa5 ♗b7.

ANALYSIS DIAGRAM

But here I only considered 31.♘xc6 ♗xc6 32.♖xc6 ♖xc6 33.♗xc6 ♕xe5 34.♕xe5 ♘xe5 35.♗b5 ♖c2, when Black is close to a draw: 36.a5 ♖xb2 37.a6 b3 38.a7 ♖a2 39.♖d8+ ♔g7 40.a8♕ ♖xa8 41.♖xa8 b2 42.♗d3 ♘xd3 43.♖b8 ♘e5 44.♖xb2.
The only correct continuation is 31.♘b3!! ♘xe5 32.♘c5! (32.♖d2!? ♘xf3 33.exf3 c5 34.♕xc7 ♖xc7 35.♖d8+ ♕f8 36.♖xf8+ ♔xf8 37.♘xc5 ♔e7 38.♔f2 leaves Black with good chances of a draw) 32...♘xf3

33.♕xc7!! ♖xc7 (33...♘xh4+ 34.gxh4 ♖xc7 35.♖d8+ ♚f8 36.♖xf8+ ♚xf8 37.♖c4) 34.♖d8+ ♚f8 35.♖xf8+ ♚xf8 36.♚xf3, with a big advantage in the endgame. However, finding this entire variation would be good grounds for immediate disqualification.

25...♚h8? An excessively abstruse move. The idea of it is to answer 26.♘xa5 with 26...f5 27.♗f3 e5 and win the game, since White does not have a check on b3. However, White is not obliged to play 26.♘xa5.

25...♕f8?! 26.h5 was also bad.

25...♕g7 was acceptable, but after 26.♘xa5 ♗xe2 27.♘xc6! ♖xc6 28.♕xe2 ♖xc1 29.♖xc1 White has a definite advantage.

The strongest was 25...c5, and now after 26.♘xa5 ♗xe2 27.♕xe2 ♖xa5 White has sufficient compensation for the pawn, but not more, while in the event of 26.♘c4 ♕f8 a very complicated position arises, with roughly equal chances.

26.♗d3! It is sad for Black to allow the exchange of the light-squared bishops, but otherwise he loses the a5-pawn without any compensation.

26...♗b7

27.♘c4

I very much wanted to play 27.♗a6, but I decided to reserve such moves for the tournament in Stavanger.

27...c5+

27...f5 could have justified Black's preceding play, but White has 28.♘bxa5 (I was intending 28.♘c5!? with the idea of 28...♗xc5 29.♘e5, which is also good) 28...♗a8 29.♘b6!.

28.♗e4 ♗a6 29.♘bxa5

White has a big advantage, but as yet it is too early to assess the position as won. Thus I don't think that Magnus, even in his very best form, has any chances here of winning against the computer.

29...♕f8 30.♗f3

But on no account 30.h5?? gxh5.

30...♖d8

30...♗d8! 31.♘b3 ♗e7!, with the idea of ...♘d7, was more resilient.

31.h5 ♗f6

And here 31...g5 was better.

32.♖xd8

Not a bad decision from the practical point of view, but 32.hxg6 hxg6 33.♘e5 was even stronger. Why?

32...♕xd8 33.♖d1 ♖d7 34.♖xd7 ♘xd7 35.h6

It is impossible to avoid making such a move, but 35.♕e4! followed by the unavoidable ♕c6 would have won, which cannot be said with confidence about the move in the game.

35...♘b6?

35...♚g8 was necessary, although after 36.b3! ♘b6 37.♘e5! Black is still on the verge of defeat.

36.♘e5 The main thing is to avoid 36.♘c6?? ♗xc4 37.♘xd8 ♘e3+.

But 36.♘xb6 ♕xb6 37.♘c6 was also quite possible.

36...♗xe5 37.♘c6

I very much liked my position, but I was not 100% certain that I was winning, and therefore the next move came as a pleasant surprise for me.

Radek Wojtaszek got various chances against Ian Nepomniachtchi, but once again the old football wisdom applied: if you don't score yourself, your opponent will.

draw by offering one!', Ian replied. 'I thought: perhaps in time-trouble he will lose his head and become confused. I reckoned that with the powerful knight on f5 I should not lose. But I underestimated the resource with the transference of the queen via d8 to f6.'

26...gxh6 27.♕g4+ ♔f8 28.♕h4

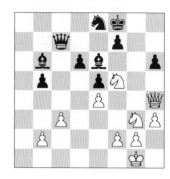

28...f6?

28...♕d8! 29.♕xh6+ ♔g8 would have won, for example: 30.♘h5 ♗xf5 31.exf5 ♕h4! 32.g3 ♕c4 33.♕g5+ ♔f8 34.f6 ♕e4. 'You rarely see such a thing! White has not even a sniff of perpetual check, and all thanks to the modest knight on e8' (D. Kryakvin).

Wojtaszek also did not notice this manoeuvre?

'I think that he saw it, but he took fright – the critically important variations looked rather risky for Black. '

29.♕xh6+ ♔g8 30.♕g6+ ♔f8 31.♕h5 ♕f7 32.♕h8+ ♕g8 33.♕h6+ ♔f7 34.♕h5+ ♔f8 35.♕h6+ ♔f7 36.♕h5+ ♔f8 37.♕h6+

Draw.

Needlessly! The assessment of the position was already +4! That is +4 with equal material...

37...♘c4 38.♘xd8 ♘e3+ 39.♔f2 ♘xc2 40.♘xf7+ ♔g8 41.♘xe5 c4 42.♗g4 ♘d4

43.♔e1

The last point that deserves a mention. Black's only trap was 43.e3?! c3 44.bxc3 bxc3 45.♔e1 ♘c2+!, but even here, after 46.♔d1 ♘xe3+ 47.♔c1, White easily wins.

43...♔f8 44.♔d1 ♔e7 45.e3 ♘b3 46.♘c6+ ♔f6 47.♘xb4 ♗b7 48.♗e2 ♘a5 49.♔d2 ♘b3+ 50.♔c3 ♘c5 51.a5 ♘e4+ 52.♔xc4 ♘xg3 53.♗d3 g5 54.fxg5+

Black resigned.

■ ■ ■

Alexander Grischuk won in normal time, gaining a second free day before the final. But the parallel match went to the 10-minute blitz. Both games with the long time-control ended in a draw without particular adventures, and then Wojtaszek missed three successive 'goal-scoring' opportunities.

**Ian Nepomniachtchi
Radoslaw Wojtaszek**
Moscow 2019 (3.4)

position after 25...♕c7

26.♗xh6?

After the tournament I enquired of Ian what this was – playing for a win or an attempt to gain a draw by perpetual check?

'No, here I could have gained a

Ian Nepomniachtchi and Alexander Grischuk at the prize-giving.
With two Russians in the final, the home crowd could be satisfied.

23.♗b2 ♗xb2 24.♕xb2 (24.♖xb2? e4) 24...♕xd3 25.♘xe5 ♕d6.
23...♘d5   24.♘xd5   ♕xd5 25.♘xd4

25...exd4 25...♕xd4 was more resilient, although even here after 26.♖e4 ♕d5 27.♗e3 White has one more piece in play.
26.♖xe8+ ♖xe8 27.♗f4 ♖e7

28.♕a4! Play over the whole board ! White provokes a weakening of the queenside and at the same time eyes the d4-pawn.
28...b6 29.c6 ♚h7 30.♖b4 ♕e6 31.♖xd4 f5 32.♗e3 g5 33.♕b4 ♖g7 34.♖d8 ♘b3 35.♗d4 ♖e7

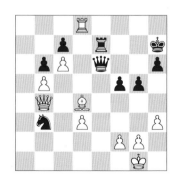

36.♕xe7+!
Black resigned. ∎

If you don't score, they score against you, and Wojtaszek conceded a kind of 'childish' goal.

Ian Nepomniachtchi
Radoslaw Wojtaszek
Moscow 2019 (3.6)

position after 18.♘fe3

18...♗c5? After the natural 18... f5 three results would have been possible, but with the move in the game Black gifted his opponent two tempi.
19.b4! ♗d6 20.c4 b6 21.a5 e4 22.♕d4 ♗e6 23.axb6 ♗xd5 24.♕xd5 ♕xd5 25.♖xd5 ♗xb4 26.♖xa6 ♘d6 27.b7 ♘xb7 28.♖b6 Black resigned.

Final

In the final between Nepomniachtchi and Grischuk, Ian held the initiative in both the main games, in the tie-break he confidently equalized with Black, and with White he outmanoeuvred Grischuk, leaving his knight off-side.

Ian Nepomniachtchi
Alexander Grischuk
Moscow 2019 (4.4)

position after 18...♕d7

19.b5 ♘a5 20.c4 ♗d4 21.♖b1 axb5 22.axb5 ♖ee8 23.c5!
There is no point in White getting involved in complications such as

The Improved Malinoise Defence

Jeroen Bosch

3...b5!?

If we limit ourselves to the 2700+ category, it has been played by Rapport, McShane and Harikrishna.

In the 1980s, the Belgian IM Michel Jadoul experimented with an unusual defence versus 1.d4. After 1.d4 he went 1...c6, which allows White to turn it into a Caro-Kann after 2.e4, but 1.d4 players will prefer 2.c4, when they would be hit by 2...b5!?. Jadoul first played his line in the Belgian town of Malines, which is why he dubbed it the Malinoise Defence. It was taken up by other players as well, most notably by Ian Rogers, who wrote an excellent article on the line for *SOS-5* (New In Chess, 2006), aptly entitled 'Thinking Sideways'. One of Black's ideas is to trade his b-pawn for White's c-pawn, which would give him a numerical advantage in the centre. However, after White's most logical response: 3.cxb5! cxb5 4.e4! ♗b7

the play resembles the Polish Defence (1.d4 b5), or even the 'St George' (1.e4 a6), even though Black has not played ...a6 yet. Although such positions may not always be easy to handle as White (remember Karpov-Miles, Skara 1980), White nevertheless should be able to obtain an opening plus.

As Rogers pointed out, things vastly improve for Black once the moves ♘f3 and ...♘f6 have been interpolated: Black then controls square e4, which means that White cannot obtain a space advantage in the centre quite so easily.

There are actually several move orders in which Black can try to reach what I would call the 'Improved Malinoise Defence'. One example is 1.c4 c6 2.♘f3 ♘f6 3.d4 b5. Another is 1.d4 ♘f6 2.c4 c6 3.♘f3 (3.♘c3) 3...b5. A third move order is:

1.♘f3 ♘f6 2.c4 c6 3.d4 b5!?

This, then, is our SOS-subject, and it is this version which has found far more favour among grandmasters. If we limit ourselves to the 2700+ category, it has been played by Rapport, McShane and Harikrishna. Now, as I mentioned, Black would like to trade his b-pawn for White's c-pawn, which means that White has two principal ways to play for an edge:

Variation A – 4.c5
Variation B – 4.cxb5

Before we investigate those moves, we should take note of the fact that the alternatives do not pose us any problems:
■ 4.♘bd2 allows Black's strategic idea; after 4...bxc4 5.♘xc4

Black has several decent responses: 5...♗a6 6.♕c2 g6 7.g3 ♗g7 8.♗g2 0-0 9.0-0 d6 10.b3 ♘bd7 11.♗b2 ♖c8 12.♖fd1 was prematurely drawn in Gonzalez-Gofshtein, Barcelona 2006. Black is equal after 12...d5 13.♘ce5 c5. With 5...g6 6.g3 ♗g7 7.♗g2 0-0 Black can opt for a healthy King's Indian set-up, while 5...e6 is perfectly playable as well.

Rapport opted for 5...d5 when, after 6.♘ce5, Black must ask himself whether 7.♘g5 is a threat. 6...e6!? (a safe reply is 6...♘e4) 7.e3 ♗d6 8.♗d3 0-0 9.0-0 ♕b6 10.♕c2 ♗a6, and Black had equalized in Eljanov-Rapport, Geneva 2017. What if White had gone for 7.♘g5? Then Black has 7...♕b6! 8.♘gxf7? (8.♘exf7 ♗b4+ 9.♗d2 0-0∓; best is 8.a3! ♗e7 9.♘exf7 0-0 10.♘e5 c5, and Black has nice initiative for the pawn) 8...♗b4+! 9.♗d2 ♘e4, and Black wins!

■ Trying to preserve the centre with 4.b3 is best answered by a fianchetto of the kingside bishop. After 4...g6 5.e3 ♗g7 Black is playing a kind of King's Indian in which White has already weakened the long diagonal.

Two examples:
– 6.♗d3 0-0 7.0-0 bxc4 8.bxc4 c5!

9.♘bd2 (9.♘c3) 9...♘c6 10.♖b1 cxd4 11.exd4 d5 and Black is already more comfortable, Clausen-Jadoul, Copenhagen 1988.
– 6.♘bd2 bxc4 7.♘xc4 0-0 8.♗b2 a5 9.0-0 ♗a6 (more flexible is 9...♕b6, with the idea of 10.♖c1 a4!) 10.♖c1 ♕b6 11.♗a3 ♖e8 12.♘e5±, Wirig-Kritz, Differdange 2007.

■ After the simple 4.e3 bxc4 5.♗xc4 the most popular reply in practice is 5...♗a6, but I prefer two different approaches:
– 5...d5 6.♗d3 e6 7.0-0 ♗e7 (7...♗d6) 8.♘c3 0-0 9.♘e5 ♘fd7 (9...c5) 10.f4 f5 11.♗d2 ♘xe5 12.fxe5 ♗a6 13.♕e2 ♗xd3 14.♕xd3 c5, and Black had a decent Stonewall in Potomak-Meduna, Ostrava 2010.
– Fianchettoing a bishop works here as well: 5...g6! 6.0-0 ♗g7 7.♘c3 0-0

8.d5 (after 8.♕e2, Rogers indicated 8...d5 9.♗d3 ♗g4 10.h3 ♗xf3 11.♕xf3 ♘bd7, and Black is fine in view of the imminent ...e5) 8...cxd5 9.♘xd5 ♘c6, and Black has an easy game, De Coninck-J.Claesen, Huy 1991.

Variation A
4.c5!?
This was Gelfand's choice when confronted with this line against Rapport. White avoids the trade of his c-pawn and gains space. Black's reply is positionally forced.
4...d6 5.cxd6 exd6
Black controls a lot of central squares with his d-, c- and b-pawns, and he has gained a certain amount of space on the queenside. On the other hand, the intrepid pawn on b5 may become a target, and with two central pawns versus one, and a half-open c-file, White

can also claim positional superiority. In practice, White now usually goes for a kingside fianchetto, which makes a lot of sense: the b-pawn has moved, which weakens the long diagonal.

6.g3
Let's briefly look at the alternatives:
■ 6.♘bd2 g6 (6...d5!?) 7.a4 b4 8.e4 ♗g7 9.♗e2 (9.♗d3) 9...0-0 10.0-0 ♖e8 11.e5, and White was slightly better in Pashikian-Gabuzyan, Yerevan 2018. But the position is tense enough.
■ Gelfand opted for 6.♗f4!?, after which 6...♗e7 is a normal and modest answer, but Rapport went for the provocative 6...♘h5!? when, after 7.♗g5 ♗e7 8.♗xe7 ♕xe7 9.e3 0-0 10.♗e2 ♘f6 11.0-0 ♗b7 12.♘bd2 ♘bd7 13.♖e1 a6 14.a4 ♘b6

the chances were balanced in Gelfand-Rapport, Prague 2019.
■ Equally logical is 6.a4 b4, but after 7.♗g5, rather than 7...h6?!, Black should have played 7...♗e7, when White has nothing special. After the text White willingly trades his bishop for the knight to gain an edge in development: 8.♗xf6 ♕xf6, and

now, rather than 9.e4?! (Jumabayev-Mikhalchenko, Tomsk 2013), White has the more subtle 9.♘bd2!, when I think that White will keep a plus, since 9...g5?! will now run into 10.e3!, while 9...g6 can be met by 10.e4. In the game Black was fine after 9...g5.

6...♗e7 7.♗g2 0-0 8.0-0 ♗b7

After 8...♘bd7 9.a4 ♗b7 10.♖e1 Black should not play the ambitious 10...♘e4?!, as in Cori-Krush, Moscow 2010. If instead she had settled for 10...a6 11.e4 ♖e8, her position would have remained very healthy.

9.♘bd2

9.♘c3 a6 (also playable are 9...b4 and 9...♘bd7) 10.♘h4 ♖e8 11.♘f5 ♗f8 12.♖e1 ♗c8!, and Black cannot be faulted for his opening play (Bruk-Kudischewitsch, Israel 2008).

9...c5 10.a4 a6 11.♖e1 ♘c6 12.e4 ♘b4! 13.♗f1

Belezky-Kritz, Lugano 2007.
And now Black could have grabbed the initiative with: **13...d5! 14.e5** 14.exd5 c4!∓ **14...♘e4 15.axb5 axb5 16.♖xa8 ♗xa8 17.♗xb5** with good play for the pawn after both 17...c4 and 17...♕b6.

Variation B

4.cxb5 The most popular reply to Black's provocative set-up. However, as I mentioned before, the fact that Black's king's knight controls square e4 is a very real advantage over the Malinoise Defence in its original form.

4...cxb5 5.e3

Sensible and solid. Clearly, the interpolation of ♘f3 ♘f6 has prevented White from taking up a more ambi-

tious position in the centre. White has several other sensible tries, of course:

■ The 'London' bishop move 5.♗f4 is entirely playable but less hard to handle. After 5...e6 6.e3 a6 7.♗d3 ♗b7 8.♘bd2 ♘c6 9.h3 ♗e7 10.♖c1 0-0 11.0-0 both sides have developed in typical fashion. White has nothing.

After 11...d6 12.e4?! e5! the play transposed to a kind of Ruy Lopez: 13.♗e3 exd4 14.♘xd4, and now 14...♘e5?! 15.♗b1 d5?! was met solidly by 16.♘f5, with some initiative for White in Kreizberg-Kudischewitsch, Tel Aviv 2002. Instead, 14...♘xd4 15.♗xd4 ♘d7, followed by moves like ...♗f6, ...♘c5 and ...♖e8 would have been very much OK for Black.

■ Nothing is gained by the early attack on b5 with 5.♕b3 a6 6.♘c3 e6 7.♗g5 ♗b7 8.e4 h6?! (8...♘c6) 9.♗xf6 ♕xf6 10.d5 exd5

11.♘xd5 (trading the knight for the bishop favours Black. The knight is a good attacking piece here, whereas the bishop is kind of shut out of the game after 11.exd5!) 11...♗xd5 12.exd5 (12.♕xd5? ♕xb2!) 12...♗c5 13.♗d3 ♕e7+ 14.♔f1 0-0 15.g3 d6, with a balanced game, Adler-Claesen, Odessa 1990.

■ I rather like 5.♗g5!?. In Fressinet-Meteuta, Plovdiv 2008, White obtained good play following 5...♗b7 6.♘bd2 a6 7.a4 b4 (Black's problems are not completely solved either after 7...h6 8.♗xf6 exf6 9.axb5 axb5 10.♖xa8 ♗xa8 11.e3 – White's edge isn't all that great, but he has a very solid position, whereas Black has some weaknesses and no real counterplay) 8.♖c1 e6?! 9.e4 h6 10.♗xf6 ♕xf6 11.♗d3 (here, 11.♘b3!? ♕d8 12.d5 is strong, too) 11...♘c6 (11...♕d8) 12.d5, and Black's position was hard to play.

No better is 5...e6 6.e4 ♕a5+ 7.♗d2 ♕b6, which also leaves White slightly better. Perhaps the best reply is 5...♘e4 6.♗h4 ♗b7 7.e3 ♕a5+ 8.♘bd2 e6

9.a3 ♘xd2 10.♘xd2 ♘c6, aiming for ...♗e7 to gradually soak up the pressure.

■ The other main move (apart from 5.e3) is 5.g3 ♗b7 6.♗g2 e6 7.0-0 ♗e7.

This position is more commonly reached via 1.d4 ♘f6 2.♘f3 e6 3.g3 b5. However, there are other move orders as well: a quite remarkable one is 1.d4 ♘f6 2.c4 e6 3.♘f3 b6

4.g3 ♗a6 5.♕a4 c6 6.♗g2 b5 7.cxb5 cxb5 8.♕d1 ♗b7, etc. I am not going to list all possible move orders, but the point is that Black has a healthy position, and that this line starting with 5.g3 can hardly be called a refutation of the Improved Malinoise Defence! This falls outside the scope of this SOS article. Just briefly, the most popular move is 8.♗g5, when Jirovsky-Navara, Karlovy Vary 2004, was drawn after 8...0-0 9.♘bd2 (9.♕d3 ♕b6 has been known to be fine for Black since Larsen-Tal, Bugojno 1978) 9...d6 (9...d5) 10.♕b3 a6 11.a4 ♗c6! 12.axb5 ♗xb5 13.♖fe1 ♘c6 14.♗xf6 ♗xf6 15.e3 d5 16.♗f1. The conclusion must be that 5.g3 poses no problems, and of the other 5th move alternatives 5.♗g5 strikes me as the most dangerous one. Let's return to the main move 5.e3.

5...a6 6.♗d3 ♗b7 There is little point in 6...e6, Thorsteins-Jadoul, Belfort 1989, which merely gives White an extra option: 7.e4.

7.0-0 e6

This is a kind of tabiya position for this SOS line. Black has developed in St George or Polish Defence fashion, but White clearly has not been able to place his pieces as actively as is possible versus these two 'more dubious' openings. Still, White has several sensible moves now. All of them are based on either exploiting Black's early queenside advance, turning the b-pawn into a target, or trying to control square e4 after all in order to take up a more aggressive position in the centre.

8.a4

Immediately targeting the b-pawn. Let's look at a few other practical examples:

■ 8.♘bd2 d5 (this prevents e3-e4, while the weakness of square c5 does not really count) 9.♘b3 ♘bd7 10.♗d2 ♗d6 11.a3 ♕e7 12.♘a5 ♗b6 13.♕b3 ♘c4! 14.♘xb7 ♕xb7 15.♗b4 ♗xb4 16.♕xb4 a5 17.♕b3 0-0 was rock-solid in Moradiabadi-Gabuzyan, St. Louis 2018.

■ 8.♕e2 (again trying to push the e-pawn) 8...d5 9.♘e5 ♘c6 10.f4!? ♗d6 11.♘d2 0-0 12.♘b3 ♘e4, with a balanced game, Lopez-Van Overdam, Netherlands 2019.

■ 8.♘c3 ♗e7?! (8...d5 makes a lot of sense and should be equal) 9.e4 b4?! 10.e5 ♘d5 11.♘e4! ♕b6?, and now White demonstrated that pawn d4 cannot be taken after 12.♘fd2! ♕xd4 13.♘c4 ♘c6 14.♗e3 ♘xe3 15.fxe3 ♕d5 16.♘ed6+, and White is winning, Thorsteins-Jadoul, Belfort 1989.

8...bxa4

According to Rogers, it is often safer for Black to take on a4 than to advance the pawn. Taking gains time, and square c4 is weakened in either case. In this concrete situation, Rogers noted, both moves are playable.

Also good is 8...b4 9.♘bd2.

and now the safe move is 9...d5.
Instead, practice saw:

■ The risky 9...♗e7!?, which provokes White into playing 10.e4! a5 11.♖e1 (White can also play for an advantage with 11.♕e2 or 11.e5 ♘d5 12.♘c4) 11...d6 12.♘b3 0-0 13.♗g5 ♘bd7 14.♕e2 h6 15.♗d2 (15.♗f4!) 15...♕b6, and now the aggressive 16.e5?! backfired after 16...♘fd7!. With 17.♗b1 White aimed for a battery, but after 17...♖e8 18.♕d3 ♘f8 Black had defended well,

and now the weakened light squares in White's camp are beginning to count, Byway-Rogers, London 1992.

■ 9...♘c6 10.e4 ♗e7 11.e5 (White has an edge after 11.♘b3 d6 12.a5) 11...♘d5 12.♘e4 0-0 13.♗g5, Zhukova-Krush, Moscow 2010, and now the tactic 13...♘xd4! would have yielded a pawn, although White has sufficient compensation after 14.♘xd4 ♗xg5 15.♘d6.

9.♘c3 ♘c6 10.♘xa4

Probably stronger is 10.♕xa4, when 10...♗b4 (10...♗e7 11.e4 ♘b4 12.♗b1 0-0 followed by ...a5 is a bit better for White) 11.♗e2 ♕b8!? (11...a5 12.♘e5±) nevertheless appears to give Black a decent enough game: 12.♘e5 (also roughly equal is 12.♗d2 ♗d6 13.♘e5 0-0 14.♖fc1) 12...♗d6 13.f4 0-0, and Black is fine. Note that White cannot take d7: 14.♘xd7? ♘xd7 15.♕xd7 ♗c6, and the queen is trapped.

10...♘b4! 11.♗b1 a5 The knight on b4 is well-placed. **12.♘c3 ♗e7 13.e4 0-0 14.♖e1** White gets no real attacking chances after 14.e5 ♘fd5, so Black is positionally fine. **14...d6 15.♗g5 ♘d7! 16.♗xe7 ♕xe7**

Black was comfortable and later won in Buhmann-McShane, Germany 2013. ■

GIBRALTAR INTERNATIONAL CHESS FESTIVAL

GIBRALTAR

16th -18th January 202[0]

UNIVERSITY O[F] GIBRALTA[R]

2020
UNIVERSITY CHESS SEMINAR

with **GM Veselin Topalov** & **IM Elisabeth Paehtz.**

Celebratory dinner with former World

Champion **ANATOLY KARPOV!**

Sharpen your game before
2020 Gibraltar Chess Festival!

♟ 3 day seminar with lunches included

♟ Guaranteed place in 2020 Gibraltar Masters

♟ Accompanying persons (not attending seminar) included on Caleta Hotel packages

PACKAGE PRICES:

SEMINAR ONLY PACKAGE: **£1,110** | SEMINAR & ACCOMMODATION PACKAGE: **£1,400**

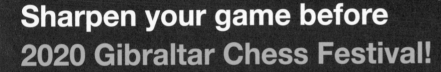

For further information please email chess@caletahotel.gi

MAXIMize your Tactics

with Maxim Notkin

Find the best move in the positions below

Solutions on page 79

1. Black to play

2. White to play

3. White to play

4. Black to play

5. White to play

6. White to play

7. Black to play

8. White to play

9. Black to play

ETERI KUBLASHVILI

A beaming Alexandra Goryachkina
(World Championship Challenger!)
at the closing ceremony together
with her younger sister Oksana.

Goryachkina shakes up hierarchy

The Women's Candidates tournament in Kazan turned into a one-horse race as Alexandra Goryachkina (20) ripped through the field to finish first with two rounds to spare. With her baffling win the Russian youngster gained the right to challenge World Champion Ju Wenjun for the highest title later this year. **KONSTANTIN LANDA** coached Russia's great hope in her biggest success to date and shares his impressions.

In Kazan, a unique city in southwest Russia on the banks of the Volga and Kazanka rivers, the Women's Candidates Tournament was contested, in which the challenger for the world chess title was determined. Until recently, the Women's World Championship cycle was a rather strange spectacle. After winning matches for the world title, each time reigning champion Hou Yifan had to start the battle practically from scratch. It is possible that for a beauty contest such a rule is absolutely normal, but it was not for classical chess.

The title of champion was awarded for victory in a knock-out competition, where one wrong move could become the last tear before leaving for home! And then a match was played with the winner of the World Cup, another knock-out competition where anything could happen... It seems surrealistic now, but that

The new leadership in FIDE did not try to reinvent the wheel, and gave women's chess full equality with men's.

was exactly how the system functioned. Of course, there were reasons for such a format, in particular the problem of finding sponsorship for a full-scale cycle.

Sadly, the strongest female player in the world, Hou Yifan, got fed up with this free-for-all, and she gave up chess, let's hope only temporarily. Fortunately, with the advent of a new leadership in FIDE, the situation changed dramatically. Their solution was simple and straightforward: they did not try to reinvent the wheel, and gave women's chess full equality with men's. Which meant a Candidates tournament to determine the Challenger to the World Champion: a double-round event with eight

players, with clear selection criteria for the tournament.

Personally, I think that this format is one of the best. It is true that there are respected trainers who hold a different point of view. For example, Ekaterina Lagno's coach, grandmaster Vladislav Tkachiev, thinks that the format is too protracted and that the tournament lost its audience after Goryachkina broke far ahead of her rivals. But here Alexandra is definitely not to blame! Look, men have played Candidates Tournaments several times, and always there has been interest right to the last round. But here, in Kazan, it just so happened that Goryachkina walked over everyone, especially in the first cycle. That said, she scored, perhaps, not so many points as she deserved by position, but by squeezing the most from her chances. Although sometimes it was largely to the 'credit' of her opponents, who went wrong at the very end of the game.

Alexandra Goryachkina
Valentina Gunina
Kazan 2019 (2)

position after 48...♖d5

49.♖f7!
White's intuition does not deceive her.

It is hard to believe that the ending after 49.♖xd5 is not winning, but according to the computer (which one can rely on in these cultured days), it is virtually a draw: 49...exd5 50.♔e3 ♗g7!! 51.♘f4 (51.♔d4?? loses to 51...f5+) 51...♔g6 52.h5+ ♔f7 53.♔f5 ♗h6 54.♘b4 ♗g5! (it is important to make the sacrifice on the square d5 – 54...d4?? 55.♘d3 ♗g7 56.♔e4 ♔e6 57.♘f4+ ♔d6 58.♔f5 and wins) 55.♘xd5 ♗c1 56.♘xf6 ♗xb2 57.g5 ♗xf6 58.gxf6 b4 with a draw.
49...♗g7 50.♘f4 ♖e5+

51.♔f3
Stronger was 51.♔d3 ♖e1 52.g5+ fxg5 53.hxg5+ ♔h7 (53...♔xg5? 54.♘g2 and wins) 54.♖b7 ♔g8 55.♖xb5.
51...♖e1 52.♖b7 ♗f1+ 53.♔e3 ♗f8 54.♖xb5 ♗d6 55.♖h5+ ♔g7 56.♘xe6+ ♔g6 57.♘d4 ♗e5
At a cost of two pawns, Black has managed to activate her pieces to the maximum.

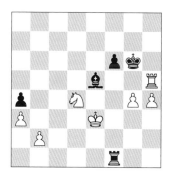

58.♘f3
Black also has good drawing chances after 58.♘f5! ♗xb2 59.♖h6+ ♔f7 60.♖h7+ ♔e6 61.♖a7 ♗xa3 62.♖xa4 ♗c1+ 63.♔e2 ♖f4 64.♖xf4 ♗xf4, and although the computer assessment

The 2019 Candidates together with FIDE president Arkady Dvorkovich: Nana Dzagnidze, Valentina Gunina, Alexandra Kosteniuk, Mariya Muzychuk, Tan Zhongyi, Kateryna Lagno, Anna Muzychuk and Alexandra Goryachkina.

here is +3, this is a bluff – the mathematically precise Lomonosov tables say it is a draw, although this still has to be earned in practice.

58...♗xb2 59.♖a5 ♗xa3 60.♖xa4 ♗c5+ 61.♔e4 ♖f2 62.h5+ ♔g7 63.♘h4 ♔h6! 64.♖a5 ♖e2+

There was a simple draw with 64...♔g5 65.h6 ♖f4+ 66.♔d3 ♖d4+ 67.♔c3 ♔xh4.

65.♔f3 ♖f2+ 66.♔g3 ♖c2 67.♘f5+ ♔g5 68.h6!

The last chance to pose problems.

68...♖c3+ 69.♔g2

69...♔xg4??

Correct was 69...♔g6! 70.♖a8 ♗e3, not fearing the rook ending with the king cut off: 71.♖g8+ ♔h7 72.♖g7+ ♔h8 73.♘xe3 ♖xe3 74.♖f7 ♖e6

75.♔g3 ♔g8 76.♖g7+ ♔h8 77.♔h4 ♖e1 78.♔h5 ♖e5+ 79.♔g6 ♖g5+ 80.♔xf6 ♖f5+, with a desperado rook and a draw.

70.h7 ♖c2+ 71.♔f1 ♖h2

71...♖f2+ 72.♔g1!!. Such a move, stepping into discovered check, can easily be missed: 72...♖xf5+ 73.♖xc5 ♖xc5 74.h8♕, with a winning position.

72.♘h4!!

Lightning from a clear sky and a study-like interference. Seeing this at move 72, in conditions of time-trouble, was not easy.

72...♔g3

72...♖xh4 73.♖a4+ ♔g5 74.♖xh4 ♔xh4 75.h8♕+; 72...♔xh4 73.h8♕+.

73.h8♕ ♖f2+ 74.♔e1 ♗b4+

75.♔d1 ♗xa5 76.♘g6 The rest is not at all interesting (1-0, 90).

Alexandra Goryachkina
Kateryna Lagno
Kazan 2019 (3)

position after 31...♔d6

Chess is a surprising game. Black has a passed pawn, with equal material, yet White has the advantage. The reason is the unequal value of the rooks in this endgame, White's being rather more active!

32.♔d4 ♖b4+ 33.♔d3 ♖b7 34.♔c4

After 34.♖a5 Black would still have to work hard to find the precise draw 34...♔c7 35.h5! ♔b6 36.♖g5 c5 37.f5 ♖d7+ 38.♔c3 ♖d4 39.fxg6 hxg6

40.hxg6 fxg6 41.♖xg6+ ♔b5 42.e5
♖e4 43.♖e6 a5!.

**34...♖b2 35.f3 ♖f2 36.♖xa7
♖xf3 37.♖xf7 ♔e6 38.♖xh7 ♖xf4
39.♔d4 c5+ 40.♔e3**

40...♖g4 Simpler is 40...♖f8 41.♖h6
(41.♖c7 ♖a8 42.♖xc5 ♖xa2=)
41...♔f7! 42.♔f4 c4 43.♔g5 ♖c8
44.♖xg6 c3 45.♖f6+ ♔e7 46.♖f1 ♔e6
with a draw.
**41.a4 ♔e5 42.♔d3 ♖g1 43.a5
♖a1 44.♖a7 ♖a4 45.a6 c4+
46.♔c3 ♔xe4 47.♖a8 ♔f5 48.a7
♔g4 49.h5! gxh5 50.♖g8+ ♔f3
51.a8♕+ ♖xa8 52.♖xa8 h4!
53.♖h8 ♔g3**

It seems that the draw is not far away,
but White finds a last, devious chance.

54.♔d2!
Wisely leaving the c4-pawn on the
board. Now many of the stalemate
ideas, which arise in the ending of R v
RP, no longer work.
54...h3??
It was essential to 'spoonfeed' the
white king on the c-pawn: 54...c3+!!
55.♔e3 c2 56.♖g8+ ♔h2 57.♖c8
♔g3!! (57...h3 loses to 58.♔f4! ♔g1
59.♖xc2 h2 60.♔g3) 58.♖xc2 h3
59.♖c8 and now Black is saved by the
only, but sufficient, move, which not
even all grandmasters know:

ANALYSIS DIAGRAM

59...♔g2! (59...h2?? 60.♖g8+ ♔h3
61.♔f2 and wins) 60.♖g8+ ♔f1
61.♔f3 h2 62.♖h8 ♔g1 with a draw.
55.♔e3 h2 56.♖g8+ ♔h3 57.♔f2
The trap is sprung and Black must
under-promote to a knight.
**57...h1♘+ 58.♔f3 ♔h2 59.♖h8+
♔g1 60.♖c8 ♘f2 61.♖xc4**
The black knight cannot remain in
the vicinity of its king and is eventually lost in the wilds of the chessboard. White won the knight and the
game (1-0, 80). Another great success
in the tournament!

Alexandra Goryachkina

Born: September 28, 1998

Career highlights

2008	Girls U-10 World Champion
2011	Girls U-14 World Champion
2011	Lyudmila Rudenko Memorial, 1st
2011	Women Grandmaster, second youngest after Hou Yifan
2012	Russian Women's Cup, 1st
2013	Russian U-19 Open, 2nd
2013	Girls U-20 World Champion
2014	Girls U-20 World Champion
2015	European Teams Women, gold on Board 3
2015	Russian Women's Cup, 1st
2015	Russian Women's Champion
2017	European Women's Championship 2nd
2017	Russian Women's Champion
2018	International Grandmaster
2019	Wins Women's Candidates Tournament

Let me make a small digression.
Goryachkina is not so well known
abroad as she is in Russia. Alexandra
was born on 28 September 1998 and
brought up in Orsk in the Southern
Ural, where Europe meets Asia. Not
the most chess-oriented town and due
to insufficient funding she was forced
to change her residence permit to
Salekhard, the only city in the world
that is located directly on the Arctic
Circle, where she received financial
support for travelling to competitions. In her 20 years Alexandra has become a multiple
world champion in different
age groups, and by the age of
13 she gained the international
grandmaster norm, becoming
the second youngest woman
grandmaster in history after
Hou Yifan. And at the age of
14 she won the world under-18
championship! She has twice
been the Russian Women's

Kazan 2019						1	2	3	4	5	6	7	8		cat. XII
															TPR
1 Alexandra Goryachkina	IGM	RUS	2522		**	½ ½	1 ½	1 ½	½ 0	1 ½	½ 1	1 1	9½	2666
2 Anna Muzychuk	IGM	UKR	2539	½ ½	**	0 ½	½ 1	½ ½	0 1	½ ½	1 1	8	2580
3 Tan Zhongyi	IGM	CHN	2513	0 ½	1 ½	**	0 ½	½ 0	½ 1	½ 1	0 1	7	2534
4 Kateryna Lagno	IGM	RUS	2554	0 ½	½ 0	1 ½	**	1 ½	½ ½	½ ½	½ ½	7	2528
5 Mariya Muzychuk	IGM	UKR	2563	½ 1	½ ½	½ 1	0 ½	**	0 ½	1 0	½ 0	6½	2498
6 Nana Dzagnidze	IGM	GEO	2510	0 ½	1 0	½ 0	½ ½	1 ½	**	0 1	1 0	6½	2505
7 Alexandra Kosteniuk	IGM	RUS	2546	½ 0	½ ½	½ 0	½ ½	0 1	1 0	**	0 1	6	2479
8 Valentina Gunina	IGM	RUS	2506	0 0	0 0	1 0	½ ½	½ 1	0 1	1 0	**	5½	2455

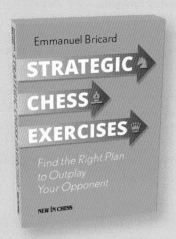
Champion. In 2018, she gained her final male grandmaster norm.

Here is a small extract from a book about Alexandra Goryachkina, describing the development of her competitive character and her early achievements: 'The debutant in the regional championship played well, and the cherished goal seemed close, but in the penultimate round a disaster occurred, which almost had dismal consequences. Before the game her opponent's side suggested an "agreed" draw, so that both girls would achieve the desired qualification. Sasha's dad rightly refused (one must fight!), and just after the opening Goryachkina won a piece, but then she blundered her queen! She could have given up in despair, but the Orsk representative won her deciding game "to order" and nevertheless qualified for the Higher League.'

Since childhood Alexandra's chess course has been guided by her father, who was a strong Soviet candidate master. Alexandra has worked with various Russian trainers, and with trainers of the Russian national team. All this is undoubtedly a big plus for a young player.

During our joint work, I have been struck by Alexandra's great tenacity, her ability to prepare well for games, her perseverance and her desire to fight to the bare kings. The final result in Kazan was also influenced by the fact that, despite the large number of excursions on the free days, we didn't go on any of them, endeavouring to prepare as well as possible for the next game. There was little time for preparation before the tournament, otherwise we would have managed to develop and practice something serious, but as it was we had to patch some 'holes' as we went along. We met only recently, and Alexandra did not always accept what I suggested. But in the end we came to a common agreement, and in some cases were able to prepare quite successfully, finding ideas 'on the fly'.

During the time that we have worked together, I have not gotten a deep insight in her daily life outside competitions, but I am fairly sure that Alexandra does not do many things that might keep her from studying chess. And this, in my opinion, is very important in top-level sport.

After the first half, when she was leading the field by one and a half points, it became clear to me that if Alexandra did not lose in the next few rounds, she would be able to maintain her lead to the end. But Alexandra not only did not lose; she also won a couple more games! Including the following great fight. Valentina Gunina was not having a great tournament, and so I expected a big battle.

Valentina Gunina
Alexandra Goryachkina
Kazan 2019 (9)
Caro-Kann, Two Knights Variation

1.e4 c6 2.♘c3 d5 3.♘f3 dxe4 4.♘xe4 ♘f6 5.♕e2 ♘xe4 6.♕xe4 ♕a5 7.♗c4 ♗f5 8.♕e2 e6 9.♘e5

The stem game went 9.0-0 ♗e7 10.♗b3 ♘d7 11.d4 0-0 12.h3 ♖fe8 13.♗f4 ♕b6 14.♖ad1 a5 15.a4 ♖ad8, with a complicated, typical Caro-Kann position, Ter Sahakyan-Grandelius, chess.com 2018.

9...♗e7 10.c3 ♗f6 11.d4 ♗xe5!? 12.dxe5 ♘d7

13.g4

Rather sharp for this position. 13.♗f4 does not pose Black any problems: 13...♘b6 14.b4 ♕a4 15.♗b3 ♕b5 16.♕xb5 cxb5 17.♗e3 ♘c4 with an equal position.

13...♗g6 14.f4 b5 15.b4?

A view of the playing room during Round 9 of the Women's Candidates tournament, when Alexandra Goryachkina faced Mariya Muzychuk (½-½, 68).

25...♗xf7! Solidity above all! **26.♗xf7 ♔xf7 27.axb5 cxb5 28.♖xa7+ ♔g6 29.♕xb5 ♖d1 30.♕c6+ ♔h7 31.♕c7 ♖g8 32.♔b3 ♖b1+ 33.♔a4 ♕e3 34.♔b5 ♖xe1 35.♖xe1 ♕xe1**

15...♕d8!
White had evidently missed this move in her calculations.
16.♗b3 ♕h4+ 17.♔d1??
Typical of Valentina's style, but out of place here. 17.♕f2 offers White chances of counterplay: 17...♕xg4 18.♗e3 0-0 19.h4; 17.♔f1!? ♕h3+ 18.♔f2 h5 19.g5 ♕h4+ 20.♔g2 ♘b6.

20.♔xd2 ♖d8+ 21.♔e3 (21.♔c1 ♕g5+ 22.♔b2 ♖d2+ winning) 21...♖d3+ 22.♕xd3 ♕h3+ and Black wins.
18.♗d2 h5 19.f5 exf5 20.e6 ♘f6 21.exf7+ ♔f8

White has managed to change the nature of the position and now both

To win by such a margin in such a tournament is the mark of a champion!

kings feel vulnerable, but the activity of the remaining pieces is clearly in Black's favour.
22.♔c1 ♘e4 23.♗e1 ♕g5+ 24.♔b2 hxg4 25.a4

Black has won a piece and later overcomes her opponent's desperate resistance.
36.c4 ♘c3+ 37.♔a5 ♕a1+ 38.♔b6 ♕g1+ 39.♔a6 ♕d4 40.♕f7 ♕d6+ 41.♔a5 ♕g6 42.♕d7 ♖f8 43.c5 f4 44.♖a6 ♕f5 45.♕d4 ♕c2 46.♔b6 ♖b8+ 47.♔c6 ♕g2+ 0-1.

After this it was sufficient simply not to 'go crazy' in the remaining games, and to play safely. There were fears in the game with Black against Lagno, but Ekaterina missed a promising continuation. And she finally lost a game in the last round, against Mariya Muzychuk. In the last few games it was hard to choose between the desire to play and the achieving of the competitive objective – first place in the tournament and qualification for the match. Therefore Alexandra did not win any more games, although she had chances. Nevertheless, the final result was impressive. To win by such a margin in such a tournament is the mark of a champion! ∎

17...♖d8 In order to play 17...0-0-0 one has to see the beautiful variation 18.♗d2 ♘xe5 19.fxe5 ♖xd2+!!

Judit Polgar

A man with many qualities

Magnus Carlsen is not a typical classical match player. **JUDIT POLGAR** examines what distinguishes the current World Champion from his great predecessors.

Throughout chess history, the term 'World Champion' has almost always referred to the strongest player on the planet at a given moment. But the way in which the outstanding players from the glorious World Champions' gallery exerted their supremacy has varied. Champions like Alekhine, Fischer, Karpov or Kasparov demonstrated their superiority over their contemporaries not only in matches to conquer and defend their titles, but also in tournaments. Several other champions had a more practical approach. They mainly specialized in matches, allowing them to prolong their reigns even when their tournament results did not manifest them as indisputable kings. One way or another, all champions that reigned for some or more years have been outstanding match players, with all the qualities required, such as a profound repertoire, a marked style and good physical and mental condition.

Seen from this perspective, a brief analysis of Magnus Carlsen's achievements reveals a paradoxical fact. Carlsen had been dominating tournament life years before he became World Champion. This domination continued (with some short intervals) after he conquered the supreme title and, at the time of writing, his domination seems to be clearer than ever. However, his last two title matches, against Karjakin and Caruana, were undecided after the classical part, and the fact that in that phase Carlsen did not appear at his leisure seems to suggest that this may not be his specialty.

This may be explained in two ways. After proving so many times in tournaments that he is, indeed, the strongest player, Carlsen probably felt huge pressure when retaining his title depended on the outcome of just one match.

The second reason for his relative weakness in matches is directly connected with an unprecedented quality: Carlsen is the first player in history to have repeatedly won World Championships in all the three popular time-controls: classical, rapid and blitz! And the feeling is that his superiority is even clearer with less time on the clock. With this in mind, it was obvious that finishing the main part of the match with an equal score would be equivalent to retaining the title in rapid or, if really necessary, blitz.

A very practical approach, although a bit demotivating. It is enough to remember the last classical game against Caruana in London. Having obtained a promising position, Carlsen offered a draw, showing that he had mentally switched to rapid mode already.

It is precisely Carlsen's extraordinary strength in blitz and rapid that I will try to highlight in this article. We will start with a blitz game, in which his strategic logic impressed me deeply.

Magnus Carlsen
Sergey Karjakin
Abidjan blitz 2019
1.c4 ♘f6 2.♘c3 e5 3.g3 ♗b4 4.e4!? A very special move order. The usual way of achieving the same struc-

ture as in the game is 4.♗g2 0-0 5.e4 ♗xc3 6.dxc3 d6 7.♕e2 ♘bd7 8.♘f3 when the knight will still have to spend a few tempi to reach a good square on e3, with either ♘h4-f5 or ♘d2-f1.

4...♗xc3 5.dxc3 d6

6.f3! The start of a smart and quicker regrouping than in the line above.

6...0-0 7.♘h3 a6 8.a4

The double pawns are strong, as they control many central squares, so White should not allow an exchange by means of the typical ...b7-b5.

8...♘bd7 9.♘f2 a5 10.♗e2

The bishop is not needed on g2 and besides White will make use of the g-file for starting an attack.

10...♘c5 11.0-0 ♗d7 12.♗e3 b6 13.♔h1 ♔h8 14.b3 ♘g8 15.g4

Preventing ...f7-f5 is just as important as preventing ...b7-b5, as it maintains White's control in the centre. White will be just in time to defend the just weakened square on f4.

15...♘e7 16.♖b1 ♘g6 17.♕d2 ♘e6 18.♘d3

With the centre absolutely stable, White does not need his knight on e3 as in the line mentioned in the

Carlsen is the first player in history to have repeatedly won World Championships in all the three popular time-controls!

introduction. White's minor pieces' regrouping is similar to that from the Sämisch Benoni, which also goes for the kingside structure.

18...♘c5 19.♖g1 ♘xd3 20.♗xd3

The bishop is much more active than it would be on g2, as it increases the pressure on f5, allowing g4-g5 without fearing ...f5 at a later moment.

20...♗c6 21.♖g3 ♕e7 22.♖bg1 ♔g8 23.♗c2 ♔h8

Everything seems to be prepared for the attack, but there is the slightly worrying aspect that the own king would also be exposed after the kingside pawns start advancing.

24.♔g2!! In blitz (and in classical chess for that matter) it is not always possible to calculate 'everything'. Intuition should also play an important part and in this case common sense suggests that before starting resolute action it would be better to evacuate the king.

24...♔g8 Black tries to do the same, but due to his more restricted space he will have to weaken his kingside, offering White a clear target.

25.♔f2 f6 26.♔e1 ♔f7 27.g5

The attack starts before the enemy king reaches safety.

27...♔e8

The kings' positions are symmetrical now, but the black one is breaking the connection of the rooks.

28.♔d1

28...♗d7

This is another moment when the relative lack of space tells, as two black pieces, the king and the bishop, compete for the d7-square. The last move was aimed to threaten ...f6-f5, thus forcing White to take a decision. But on the other hand reconnecting rooks becomes improbable in the near future, offering White a material superiority on the kingside. If 28...♔d7 White could develop his attack gradually, starting with 29.h4.

29.gxf6 ♕xf6 A necessary concession as after 29...gxf6 30.h4 the rooks' intrusion through the g-file would be decisive. For instance: 30...♘xh4? 31.♖g7 ♖f7?! 32.♖g8+ ♖f8 33.♗h6 and White wins.

30.♗g5 ♕e6 31.h4 ♖f7 32.h5 ♘f8

White has perfect mobilization, while Black's coordination is awful. But instead of searching for a forcing continuation of the attack, Carlsen makes one more prophylactic move:

33.♔c1!! Yes, this is a blitz game and yes, the engines completely agree with this move!

33...g6 This offers White another target, but Black had no ways of regrouping properly. For instance, if 33...♗c6 34.♗d3 followed by ♗f1-h3 and the black king cannot reach b7.

34.f4

Starting to destroy Black's central fortress.

34...exf4 35.♗xf4 ♗c6 36.e5 dxe5 37.♗xe5 ♖e7 38.hxg6! hxg6

38...♕xe5 39.g7 wins.

39.♗xg6+

A typical human decision. Carlsen saw a forced win and did not ask for more. Engines think differently and consider 39.♖e3 'even better'.

39...♘xg6 40.♖xg6 ♕xe5 41.♖g8+ ♔f7 42.♕f2+ ♔e6 43.♖1g6+ ♔d7 44.♕d2+ ♗d5 45.♖xa8 ♕e1+ 46.♕xe1 ♖xe1+ 47.♔d2 ♗xa8 48.♔xe1

and White won (1-0, 68).

This blitz game is remarkable for its general strategic character from the early opening on until White obtained a decisive material advantage. The tactical nuances were rather simple,

But in the next rapid game, Carlsen took a series of outstanding concrete decisions.

**Ian Nepomniachtchi
Magnus Carlsen
Abidjan rapid 2019**

position after 28.♕e2

The position is very sharp as both players have a far advanced passed pawn. The black one is safely blocked, so Carlsen decides to send his colleague to help.

28...e4!? 29.h4?

Generally a useful move, apparently clearing some space for the king with gain of time before taking a decision regarding the e-pawn, but in fact the decisive mistake.

29.♗xe4? ♗h3 is bad for White as if the queen will be forced to blockade the f-pawn after ♕xf1 he would be awfully passive, while 30.♗g2 ♗xg2+ 31.♔xg2 ♕xd5+ wins the knight.

The correct answer was 29.♕xe4! ♗a6 30.♕e6! ♗xf1 31.♗xf1 ♔h8 32.h4 ♕f3+ 33.♔h2 Due to the threat ...b6-b7-b8, Black would now or soon have to force a draw by a perpetual with ...♗xh4.

29...e3!!

A fantastic move, showing that Magnus feels the momentum. I would commend his calm, self-confidence and the way he enjoys the game, giving the impression that he is flying.

In rapid chess one would expect the automatic bishop retreat, of course.

30.hxg5

30...♖e8!! Such quiet moves when a piece down are easy to overlook. Black simply defends the pawn on e3, paralyzing White. **31.♔h2** There is no other reasonable move. **31...♗g4!** Highlighting the fact that the queen is a bad blocking piece. It is also interesting to notice that the bishop delivers the killing blow from its initial square! **32.♕xg4 e2**

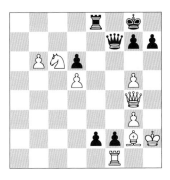

Truly amazing pawns!

33.b7 ♕xb7 34.♖xf2 e1♕

It is not very common that a game continues for 15 more moves when one of the players has two queens. Carlsen must have greatly enjoyed coordinating their actions.

35.♕f5 ♕e3 36.♖f3 ♕e2 37.♘d4 ♕e5 38.♕g4 ♕bxd5 39.♘f5 ♕de6 40.♕h5 ♕g6 41.♕g4 h5 42.♕c4+ d5 43.♕b5 ♕xg5 44.♕d7 h4 45.♖f1 hxg3+ 46.♔g1 g6 47.♗xd5+ ♔h8 0-1.

Conclusion

■ In blitz games it is important to keep your strategic orientation and listen to your intuition.

■ In addition, in rapid games you have the time to take radical decisions when the critical moment arises. ■

1. Sethuraman-Iturrizaga
Dubai 2019

39...♖d6! Clearing the e-file as well as the d4-square. **40.♖f2 ♖d1+** White resigned. More attractive was 40.♕f2 ♗d4! with mate on e1 as the point.

2. Lei Tingjie-Guramishvili
China 2019

23.♖xg7! ♔xg7 24.♖g1+ ♔h8 25.♕h6 ♖g8 25...♗g5+ 26.♖xg5 f5 27.♘e6. **26.♖xg8+ ♔xg8 27.♘f6+ ♗xf6 28.♗xh7+ ♔h8 29.♗f5+** Black resigned.

3. Ponomariov-Beerdsen
Bundesliga 2019

23.♗xf7+! ♔xf7 24.♕c4+ ♔e7 If 24...♔f8 25.♖xd7! ♕xd7 26.♗c5+ Black has to give up the queen. **25.♗c5+ ♔f6** 25...♔d8 26.♕f7 also with mate. **26.♗d4+** Black resigned.

4. Sarakauskas-McShane
England 2019

21...f4! 22.♘xf4 ♖xf4 23.♗xf4 ♗xg2! Possible as the h4-knight is not attacked now. **24.♘xg2** 24.♕c3 ♕h3, threatening 25...♘f3+. **24...♘f3+ 25.♔h1 ♘xd2** and wins.

5. Shyam-Pranav
Dubai 2019

32.♘xg4! fxg4 33.♗c3 ♕d8 33...♕f7 34.♗h7 mate would be just ludicrous. **34.♗h7+ ♔f7 35.♕g6+! ♘xg6 36.hxg6** Mate!

6. Yeletsky-Ofitserian
Sochi 2019

24.♘f6 ♖xe2 25.♖he1! ♖e5 25...♖xe1 26.♖xe1 ♖h8 27.♖e8+ ♔g7 28.♖xh8 ♔xh8 29.♕h6#. **26.♘xh7+ ♔g7 27.♘f6 ♕e7 28.♖xe5 dxe5 29.♕f2!** wins (29...♘d3 30.♘xh5+).

7. Iturrizaga-Aditya
Sharjah 2019

26...♘g4! 27.g3 27.fxg4 ♖xf1+ 28.♔xf1 ♖f8+ 29.♔g1 ♕e1+ 30.♔h2 ♖f1 mates. **27...♕xg3+ 28.♔g2 ♖xf3! 29.♔xf3** 29.♕xg3 ♖xg3+ 30.♔h1 ♖d5 doesn't help. **29...♖d1+** White resigned in view of 30.♖f1 ♖xf1+ 31.♔xf1 ♘h2+ 32.♔g1 ♘f3+.

8. Zhukova-A.Vovk
Gallipoli 2019

29.f6 ♖xf6 30.♕g5+ ♔f7 was a draw. Better is **29.♖g3+ ♔h8 30.f6!** ♖xf6 After 30...♕xf6 31.♖f3 ♕g7 32.♖xf8+ ♕xf8 33.♕xe5+ the king won't survive; 30...♕c5+ 31.♔h1 ♕c2 fails to 32.f7. **31.♕xe5! ♕f8 32.♖f3 ♔g7 33.g4!** and 34.g5 wins.

9. Vokhidov-Adly
Dubai 2019

37...♖f8! Gaining access to f4 for his queen. **38.♗f1 ♖xf2+ 39.♘xf2 ♕f4+ 40.♔e1 ♕e3+ 41.♕e2** If 41.♔d1 ♕xf2 42.♕xe6+ the black king hides on h6. **41...♗c4!** White resigned as after 42.♕xe3 dxe3, nothing can stop ...♖xf1 mate.

When in Scotland...

Magnus Carlsen wins in a whisky distillery

Two historical documents united whisky and chess at the Lindores Abbey Chess Stars. **DIRK JAN TEN GEUZENDAM** tasted the 'aqua vitae' and saw the World Champion win a barrel full of promise.

Magnus Carlsen's only win, with the white pieces against Vishy Anand, sufficed for overall victory in the Lindores Abbey Chess Stars.

Now that chess is increasingly promoted as 'an educational tool' and top stars are younger and physically fitter than ever, the association of chess and whisky feels like turning back the clock several decades to when you could easily imagine two distinguished gentlemen engrossed in a game while sipping a dram. Yet, the Lindores Abbey Chess Stars was held in a whisky distillery and the presence of four of the world's best players, surrounded by all the game transmission techniques that we have become accustomed to, definitely gave it the feel of a slightly

unusual but perfectly modern chess competition.

So, how did whisky and chess come together at a distillery not that far away from Dundee, where, in 1867, one of the first tournaments of the modern chess age was held? (In case you forgot, Neumann won, ahead of Steinitz.) Perhaps to begin with, it should be said that very little is left of Lindores Abbey. Founded in 1191, the abbey saw several prosperous centuries, but like so many other Catholic monasteries it did not survive the Reformation that dramatically changed the religious landscape on the British Isles.

However, some of the ruins (a wall here and there) were ingeniously incorporated into the brand-new whisky distillery that was built on the site of the monastery and has been operational since 2017. And although it has only been open for two years, it has already become a favourite destination for whisky lovers, because a document from 1494 seems to provide proof that the Lindores monks were the first to produce whisky (aqua vitae, water of life, in the document) in Scotland. As the famous whisky writer Michael Jackson noted: 'For the whisky-lover, it is a pilgrimage.' At the same time, it should be mentioned that there is no whisky yet, since whisky should mature at least three years and a day, and it might well take several more years before the first Lindores Abbey whisky appears on the market. In the meantime, they do sell a 'spirit drink with herbs and spices' that they say is something in-between gin and whisky. And for the chess tournament, a limited special edition of 500 bottles of this 'Aqua Vitae' was bottled.

Big chess lover

Another historical document that played a role in causing the first visit of World Champion Magnus Carlsen to Scotland was a late 15th century inventory of the abbey, which mentions 'Two pairs of Thabills wt thair men', which has been interpreted as meaning that the monks had 'two chess boards with their pieces'.

But two historical documents do not necessarily make a chess tournament; for that, the two Russian investors in the distillery were needed, one of whom is a big chess lover. Already last year he had hoped to promote their venture with a chess tournament involving Magnus Carlsen, but only this year did the World Champion find time in his packed schedule. The other players invited for the two-day rapid event were teetotallers Vishy Anand and Ding Liren. And the fourth player would be determined by the outcome of the first-round pairing Grischuk-Karjakin of the Moscow Grand Prix that took place at the same time. Sergey Karjakin lost that mini-match and immediately flew to Scotland, where, just like the other players and guests, he was accommodated in a splendid country home close to the venue.

Very, very cold

The presence of the World Champion and former World Champion Anand attracted hundreds of Scottish chess fans, and you got the impression that there would have been even more if the number of tickets had not been limited due to space restrictions. Carlsen was obviously the favourite to win, and

there was no question about whether he was motivated to live up to expectations. Curiously enough, the games were played immediately next to the huge copper vessels in which the whisky is distilled, but everything was done to create a comfortable and quiet environment, which is why the hosts were shocked when, on the very first day, the World Champion criticized the playing conditions, saying, 'It was very, very cold, and because of this I didn't really enjoy it.' A couple of small heaters were brought in, but at the start of the second day a more befitting solution was found: before the chess started, the distilling process (which had been interrupted because the vessels get really hot)

A late 15th century inventory of the abbey mentions 'Two pairs of Thabills wt thair men'.

was started for a couple of hours, which not only created a comfortable temperature, but also a soft and soothing whisky smell that may have inspired Carlsen in the following game.

NOTES BY
Anish Giri

**Magnus Carlsen
Sergey Karjakin**
Lindores 2019 (5)
Queen's Pawn Opening

1.d4 ♘f6 2.♘f3 d5 3.g3
A curious move order that is almost never better than the Réti, 1.♘f3/2.g3, except for that one line that Karjakin plays: 1.♘f3 ♘f6 2.g3 c5 3.♗g2 ♘c6.
3...g6

Sergey Karjakin fortunately has enough overview to get to a familiar position. The more principled move would be to develop the c8-bishop.
4.♗g2 ♗g7 5.0-0 0-0 6.c3

This was made popular by the efforts of Vladimir Kramnik, who at some point got possessed by the idea of trying to play his Black repertoire with an extra tempo with White.
6...♘bd7 7.♗f4 c5 8.♘e5 ♕b6
8...♘h5!? is a standard reply in such cases.
9.♕b3 cxd4 10.♕xb6 ♘xb6 11.cxd4

The knight is not well placed on b6 here, as it can be easily dominated by the little b3-pawn, so that White is usually slightly better. It is also very important that White has stabilized his knight on e5 and that Black will have to do the same with his e4-knight if he wants to equalize.
11...♘e4
Starting with 11...♗f5!? would probably have been more clever: 12.♘c3 (12.♖c1 ♖fc8!) 12...♘e4!.
12.♖c1

12...♘d6?! I don't see the excitement about the f6-knight being on d6. If only it was the b6-knight. 12...♗f5! was stronger and more natural.

13.♘c3?! A more sophisticated move was called for, e.g. 13.h4!? or 13.a4!?; but the ...♘f5/ ...g5 operation in my next note is really hard to anticipate.

13...♗e6?! Here 13...♘f5!? would justify the knight manoeuvre quite a bit. The ensuing position is a complete mess: 14.e3 g5 15.♗xg5 f6 16.g4 ♘d6 17.♘xd5 ♘xd5 18.♗xd5+ e6. God knows what is going on here.

14.a4 a5

15.h4 15.♘f3!? was strong, threatening 16.♗xd6, and after 15...♘e4 16.♘b5 an invasion on c7 is going to be hard to meet (16...♗d7 17.♖c7).

At the same time White can go b3 to kill all Black's counterplay attempts whenever he wants to.

15...♖fc8 16.b3 White is playing very harmoniously and enjoys a stable advantage.

16...♖c7

17.♘b5?! More nuanced play was necessary to exploit White's positional advantage. A slower time-control would have made it more likely for Magnus to spot that the a5-pawn is rather lonely: 17.♗d2! ♖ac8 (17...♘f5 is a natural attempt to look for counterplay: 18.♘b5 ♖xc1+ 19.♖xc1 ♘xd4 20.♘xd4 ♗xe5 21.♘xe6 fxe6, and now 22.e4! would yield White an advantage, since he would pick up the a5-pawn eventually and keep the bishop pair) 18.♘a2, and the a5-pawn is falling.

17...♖xc1+ 18.♖xc1 ♘xb5 19.axb5 ♖c8 20.♖c5

White probably thought that e4 was a serious threat here, but it turns out there are various ways to deal with it. Positionally speaking, on the other hand, the ♘b5 operation was a disaster, since the b6-knight will have a bright future after the inevitable push ...a4.

20...♚f8 21.e4

21...a4!? A good simplifying operation, inviting messy complications. Seeing his stable advantage disappearing, White picks up the gauntlet.

22.exd5!? 22.bxa4 ♘xa4 23.♖xc8+ ♗xc8 24.exd5 ♘c3 25.b6 ♘a4 is clearly safe for Black.

22...♖xc5 There were other ways of queening the pawn, but play would remain complex and practically speaking totally unclear in all cases. After 22...a3!? 23.dxe6 a2 24.♘d7+ ♚e8 25.♘xb6 a1♕+ 26.♚h2 Black would have had the extra option of keeping the rooks with 26...♖d8!, when White has more things to worry about than in the game.

23.dxc5 a3 24.dxe6 a2 25.♘d7+ ♚e8 26.♘xb6 a1♕+ 27.♚h2 ♗e5

Immediately after the game Magnus Carlsen and his father Henrik began discussing if the sacrifice against Sergey Karjakin was a draw or if there were even chances to win.

Magnus Carlsen won the first Lindores Abbey Chess Stars, but with a smaller margin than he might have hoped for. In fact, he had to fight to survive a difficult final-round endgame against Ding Liren to win at all. The decisive game proved to be his encounter as White with Vishy Anand, the only game out of six that he won. Victory meant not only an undisclosed appearance fee, but also a barrel of whisky – or rather, a barrel of what one day will be a fine whisky. He still has some years to make up his mind about whether he will want to have it shipped to Norway.

NOTES BY
Anish Giri

Magnus Carlsen
Vishy Anand
Lindores 2019 (3)
Nimzo-Indian Defence, Rubinstein Variation

Despite apparently total chaos, the engine assesses the position as equal. White is obviously in very little danger, given all the fortress resorts available to him if things went wrong. That said, it is also hard to win.
28.♗e3 fxe6 28...♗d4 runs into 29.c6!. **29.♗xb7 ♗d4!**

37.g4 ♕d4 38.♘f1 h5 39.gxh5 gxh5 40.♘g3 e5 41.♘e4 ♕c4 42.♘g5 ♔b8 43.♗e4 ♕e2 44.♗f5 e4 45.♘xe4 ♕c4 46.♘g3 ♕xc6+ 47.♗e4 ♕f6 48.♘xh5 ♕xh4 49.♘g3

1.d4 ♘f6 2.c4 e6 3.♘c3
Carlsen has been experimenting with the Nimzo-Indian off and on, in particular in this rapid tournament in Scotland, where he opened his first game against Ding Liren with the good old Sämisch Variation (after 3...♗b4 4.a3 ♗xc3 5.bxc3 b6 6.f3).
3...♗b4 4.e3 0-0 5.♗d3 d5 6.cxd5 exd5 7.♘ge2

30.♘c4!? White keeps the game going, but doesn't have enough resources to queen his queenside pawns. After 30.c6 ♗xe3 31.c7 ♗xf2 32.c8♕+ ♔f7 the threat of 33...♕g1+ gives Black enough time to pick up the b6-knight, with a draw.
30...♗xe3 31.♘xe3 ♕b2 32.♔g2 ♕xb3 Also possible was 32...♕d4 33.c6 ♔d8. **33.b6 ♕b5 34.♗f3 ♔d8 35.b7 ♔c7 36.c6 ♕b4**
White would love to see his knight land on d7, but that is not on the menu at all, so the position is a draw.

Draw. Interestingly, if White didn't have the b7-pawn, I assume it would be a draw as well, with the famous ♗g2/♘e4 fortress set-up.

■ ■ ■

This is a popular and ambitious set-up with many finesses. White is hoping to eventually prepare f3-e4, while Black usually aims to prevent this with (b6)-c5.
7...♖e8 8.♗d2

CHESSBASE MAGAZINE

8...b6!?

Vishy Anand is toying with the move order a little, seemingly managing to confuse the World Champion.

At Norway Chess 2017, 8...♗f8 9.0-0 b6 10.♖c1 c5 11.♘f4! (an improvement by Carlsen over a blitz-game Jobava-Karjakin in 2016) 11...♗b7 12.♕f3 yielded Carlsen a nice position against Karjakin, since White aims to finish his development with ♖fd1 and start putting pressure on the d5-pawn (1-0, 44).

9.0-0

In connection with what Carlsen wants to do, given the early ♗d2 and the obsession with the move ♖c1, this is already inaccurate. 9.♖c1!? would prevent ...♗d6. Strangely enough, despite having played this variation a few times, the World Champion decided to skip this rather pretty finesse.

9...♗d6!? 10.♖c1?!

This move and, especially, the next one are hard to explain, seeing that White fails to achieve anything here. 10.♘f4 deserves attention.

10...c5

Black gets ...♗d6 and ...c5 without having to prevent ♘b5 with ...a6. He is doing very well now.

11.♘b5?!

White is a move too late again, and unless it is followed by dxc5, this move seems pointless. I imagine White was hoping that Black would go for the very unnecessary ...a6 and then ...♗d6, but Vishy is far too cultured to do this and the b5-knight far too misplaced.

11...♗f8 12.f3

12.dxc5 bxc5 would be a natural follow-up, but since 13.b4 fails to 13...a6, and 13.♗c3 ♘bd7 14.♕d2! a6 15.♗a5! is too sophisticated, White thought better of this.

12...♘c6

Black is better now. He can maintain the central tension for as long as he wants and White failed to get the d2-bishop activated via e1. His pieces are clumsy. That said, White is obviously still solid and there are many pieces left on the board, so the game goes on.

13.♔h1 ♗b7 14.a3 g6

Both sides are making small improvements, which doesn't help White's situation, because he is struggling with both a lack of space and a dearth of clear-cut ideas.

15.♗b1

15...♖c8

15...♗a6!? was an interesting option, but the follow-up 16.♕a4 ♘a5!? is rather hard to see. Objectively, though, White is in a bit of trouble here, with some pins and potential overloads.

16. ♗a2 a6

Black would have been better off postponing ...a6. It is not necessary at all to send the knight back to the better square. Also, it is nice for Black to have the ...♗a6 option.

Stronger was 16...♕d7!.

17.♘bc3 ♗g7

He could have forced matters with 17...♗h6!?, because the e4-push leads to simplifications that don't look too good for White.

18.dxc5 bxc5 19.♗e1

White has managed to make his play look logical: he has manoeuvred one bishop to a2, and now the other one goes to h4. But he took too much time and Black's set-up is more harmonious.

19...d4?

Opening the a2-g8 diagonal and inviting some cheapos. Not good. 19...♖xe3 20.♗f2 ♖e8 21.♗xc5 ♘e5, followed by some further knight jumps, would give Black a lot of play for his isolated pawn.

Magnus Carlsen was visibly touched by a surprise gift from the sponsors, an amber chess set they bought from the family of Mikhail Tal. Tal's son Gera (left) came from Israel to Scotland to hand him the set.

20...♘e5! 21.exd4 cxd4 22.♖xc8 ♕xc8 23.♘xd4 ♘c4 gives Black good compensation for the pawn. He gets the bishop pair, and with the remaining knight ready to jump to e3, he would have easy play and nothing to worry about.

21.♗xf7+! ♔xf7 22.♕b3+

22...♔f8? Speaking of chess laws, there is no official rule that once a cheapo has been missed, a player is forced to collapse immediately, although this rule is unfortunately followed far too often at every level.

22...c4! would make things even messier.

23.♕xb7 ♖xe3?

23...dxe3! would have yielded Black better chances to survive. There is a hint of counterplay with such an advanced pawn, even though it is safely blocked for now.

24.♘g3 ♘ce5 25.♗d2 ♖d3 26.♘e4 ♖b8 27.♕d5

Once the queen comes out, the smoke will clear and Black will be totally lost.

27...♖xd2 28.♘xd2 ♘d3 29.♖c2 ♕e7 30.♘e4 ♘f4 31.♕c4

Black resigned. ∎

However, 19...c4! was the strongest option, when White struggles to equalize: 20.♗f2 (20.♘f4 ♖xe3 21.♘fxd5 ♖d3 22.♘xf6+ ♕xf6 23.♕a4 ♘e5

ANALYSIS DIAGRAM

and it is enough to look at the pieces to realize that things are not going well for White. Black is rolling: 24.♗g3 ♖d4!, and the famous octopus is coming towards d3) 20...♗h6, asking White some unpleasant questions.

20.♘a4 20.♘e4!? might have been stronger, but the all-seeing World Champion probably already saw the blunder coming.

20...♘d7?

The laws of chess are such that missing a cheapo can often put paid to all your previous efforts.

Lindores 2019					1	2	3	4		cat. XXII
										TPR
1	**Magnus Carlsen**	IGM	NOR	2861	∗ ∗	½ ½	½ ½	1 ½	3½	2834
2	**Ding Liren**	IGM	CHN	2805	½ ½	∗ ∗	1 ½	½ 0	3	2795
3	**Sergey Karjakin**	IGM	RUS	2752	½ ½	0 ½	∗ ∗	1 ½	3	2813
4	**Vishy Anand**	IGM	IND	2774	0 ½	½ 1	0 ½	∗ ∗	2½	2749

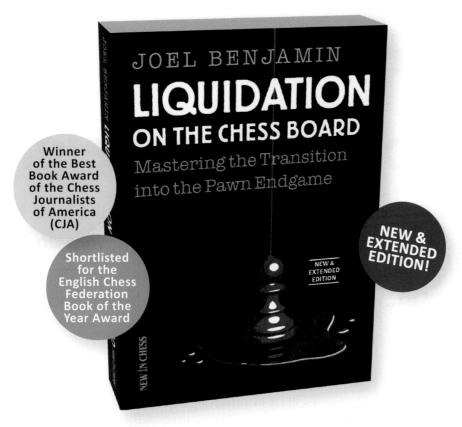

JOEL BENJAMIN
LIQUIDATION
ON THE CHESS BOARD
Mastering the Transition into the Pawn Endgame

Winner
of the Best
Book Award
of the Chess
Journalists
of America
(CJA)

Shortlisted
for the
English Chess
Federation
Book of the
Year Award

NEW &
EXTENDED
EDITION!

NEW IN CHESS

In this New and Extended Edition, three-time US Champion Joel Benjamin has
added dozens of new examples, besides making other additions and corrections.

"I have, until now, never seen a collection of exercises on the theme of transition into the endgame, let alone with such precise solutions as Benjamin presents here."
Dennis Calder, FIDE Instructor

"The book works quite addictively. It's dealing with one of the big moments of uncertainty in practical chess."
GM Matthew Sadler

"Strongly recommended. In transitions into pawn endgames a lot can be gained and a lot can be lost."
Schach Magazin 64

"An excellent guide to a difficult theme that has been badly served

in chess literature. If you are really serious about improving your chess, you should work on your Benjamin!"
IM Frank Zeller, Magazine Schach

"Entertainment is never far away. The material, which feels very fresh, provides an impressive series of easily digestible lessons."
Sean Marsh, CHESS Magazine

"An instructive work for players at any level above beginner – but it's not a dry endgame manual. The games contain some beautiful ideas and overall I found the book very entertaining.' – GM Daniel King**

"Benjamin tackles one of the most important (and underappreciated) aspects of

endgame practice." – **GM Daniel Naroditsky, Chess Life Magazine**

"An excellent new book. The theme of the right exchange is underrepresented in chess literature and Joel Benjamin manages to highlight its importance by investigating the transition into a pawn endgame in deep detail."
GM Karsten Müller, author of 'Fundamental Chess Endings'

"The book is anything but dry. Benjamin is excellent at explaining not only the intricacies of specific positions, but also useful practical guidance for general endgame play. I felt that I gained a lot from these instructions." – **GM David Smerdon, Chess.com**

paperback | 304 pages | €27.95 | available at your local (chess)bookseller or at newinchess.com | a **NEW IN CHESS** publication

MVL scales new heights

Magnus Carlsen's domination in blitz is seriously challenged by Maxime Vachier-Lagrave. The 'Frenchman with three recent wins against the World Champion' is the new leader in the blitz world rankings. **MAXIM DLUGY** examines what makes MVL such a phenomenal speed chess player.

While Magnus Carlsen has been blazing through traditional time-control tournaments this year, Maxime Vachier-Lagrave, or MVL, as the Frenchman is commonly known in chess circles, has shown that there is another candidate for the lead position in blitz. With his notable victory in the Blitz part of the Côte d'Ivoire leg of the Grand Chess Tour – the first leg of the 2019 Tour – where he scored 12 from 18, MVL had come close to Carlsen's rating. A few weeks later, he closed that gap and tore way ahead of the classical World Champion by winning the blitz at the start of Altibox Norway Chess with a stunning 7½/9 points, 1½ points ahead of Carlsen and Aronian.

MVL has now beaten Magnus in the last three official blitz games they played against each other, while also threatening to become the official number 1 blitz player in the world, since he is almost 30 points ahead of Magnus on the live rating list.

What makes MVL shine? What is the spark that got him to his highest-ever live blitz rating of 2947.8 points?

I will try to answer those questions by analysing his blitz games from the Ivory Coast tournament in Abidjan.

To begin with, let's look at two of MVL's notable blitz strengths in the following game against Wesley So.

**Maxime Vachier-Lagrave
Wesley So**
Abidjan Blitz 2019 (1)
Catalan Opening Accepted

1.♘f3 d5 2.g3 c5 3.♗g2 ♘c6 4.d4 e6 5.0-0 ♘f6 6.c4 dxc4 7.dxc5 ♕xd1 8.♖xd1 ♗xc5 9.♘bd2 c3 10.bxc3 0-0 11.♘b3 ♗e7 12.♘fd4 ♘xd4 13.cxd4 ♘d5 14.♗d2 f5 15.♖ac1 b6

16.♗xd5 Officially a novelty, though not a very impressive one. White has done well with 16.f3 instead, although Black seems to have reasonable play if he meets the rook on c7 in timely fashion with 16...♗d7 17.e4 ♘f6 18.♖c7 ♖fc8 19.♖dc1 ♖xc7 20.♖xc7 ♗d8 21.♖c1 ♖c8.

16...exd5 17.♖c7 ♗d8 18.♖c2 ♗a6

White's main problem in this position is that, besides the advantage of the two bishops, Black has good access to the c4 outpost for his bishop, so it is important for White to start thinking about equalizing.

19.♗f4 ♗e7

20.♖dc1?

A significant inaccuracy, giving Black free time to minimize potential counterplay by White.

It was important to displace Black's rook with 20.♖c7 ♖f7 21.♖c2!, anticipating Black's bishop going to c4 and planning to meet it with f3 and e4. In that case, White could successfully fight for equality.

20...♗a3! Kicking the rook from the c-file. **21.♖b1 ♖ac8 22.♘a1!**

We are being shown one of MVL's key blitz traits: an excellent ability to spot good knight moves. Look for them in his games, and in your own, and you will significantly improve your blitz strength. The problem is that knight moves are curved and therefore not so easy to spot in time-trouble. The solution is to always be alert to finding a cool knight move and look for them whenever possible.

22...♖fe8 23.♗e5 ♔f7 24.♔f1

It was a little more accurate to use the strength of the a1-knight and to play f3, followed by ♔f2, seeing that Black cannot win the e-pawn since his bishop would be hanging on a3.

24...g5

25.♖b3 White is in a tough position, as Black's two bishops have great long-term potential and it's hard to decide on the right plan of defence.

Magnus Carlsen could not know that his first game against Maxime Vachier-Lagrave in Abidjan would be the first of three consecutive losses against the Frenchman.

A possible approach was to bring the knight in with 25.♖d2 ♔e6 26.♘c2 ♗e7 27.♘b4 ♗c4 28.♘d3, although Black is still quite a bit better, since he will advance his queenside pawns with the support of his c4-bishop.

25...♗e7 26.♖bc3 ♖xc3 27.♖xc3 ♖c8?

This should have cost Black all his advantage. He should have kept his

rook (because White's one is passive behind the c4-bishop) and should have played 27...♗c4! 28.♘b3 a5, with a huge advantage.

28.♖xc8 ♗xc8 29.♘b8 ♗d8

30.♘c2?

Wesley's bluff works. This was a

critical moment, because MVL had to see how to extricate the bishop after taking on a7.

There was a way! After 30.♗xa7! ♗c7 31.♘c2 ♔e6 32.♘b4 ♗d7 33.♔e1 ♗b5 34.♔d2 ♔d6 35.f4 gxf4 36.gxf4 ♗c4 37.e3 ♔d7 38.a4 ♔c8 39.a5 bxa5 40.♘c2 White is still worse, but breaking through would be extremely different, if at all possible.

Maxime Vachier-Lagrave has excellent abilities to spot good knight moves.

30...a5 31.♔e1 ♗a6 32.♔d2 ♗c4 33.a3 ♔e6 34.♘e3 ♗b5 35.♘d1

Take note of how MVL uses his knight to wriggle free.

35...♗e7 36.♘c3 ♗c6 37.a4 ♔d7 38.♔c2 ♗b4

39.♘b5!?

In lost positions, deciding on which bad endgame to settle for is always the hardest choice to make. Here we come to MVL's second noteworthy blitz strength – tenacity. Like a good poker player, he optimizes his bad hand, letting his opponent solve the tougher problem. Instead of going into an opposite-coloured bishop endgame in which Black's winning chances approach 100% and White's are zero, MVL offers So the consideration that going into the same-coloured bishop ending might not be winning. And he tricks him into keeping the two bishops.

39...♗e1 40.f3

40...g4

Black easily wins the endgame after 40...♗xb5 41.axb5 g4!, fixing the h2-pawn, which Black can then easily pick up.

41.fxg4

It's interesting that once MVL has decided on his bluff, he doesn't go back on it and try ♘c3. He is convincing Wesley that trading on b5 is not good enough. Amazingly, Wesley buys it!

41...fxg4? 42.♗f4 ♗f2 43.♔d3

43...♗g1?

After this it will be difficult to get a clearly winning position again.
A simple win could still be achieved as follows: 43...♗xb5+ 44.axb5 ♗g1 45.♔g5 ♗xh2 46.♗h4 ♗g1 47.♗f6 h5 48.♗h4 ♗f2 49.♔c3 a4 50.♔b4 ♔e6 51.♔xa4 ♗xd4 52.♔b4 ♗f6, and Black wins.

44.♘c3!

44...♗xh2?

After this, Black will struggle to survive. The Spassky-Fischer ...♗xh2 comes to mind here. The bishop cannot get back without the loss of a few key pawns. Black had to keep the bishop on g1 and manoeuvre

Abidjan blitz 2019		cat. XXI
		TPR
1 Vachier-Lagrave	12	2890
2 Carlsen	11½	2858
3 Nakamura	11	2847
4 Nepomniachtchi	10½	2822
5 Karjakin	9½	2789
6 So	8½	2747
7 Ding Liren	8½	2741
8 Wei Yi	7½	2713
9 Topalov	5½	2628
10 Amin	5½	2632
18 rounds		

the other one to a6 first. Then, after 44...♗b7 45.♗e5 ♗xh2 46.e4! dxe4+ 47.♘xe4 ♔e6 48.♘g5+ ♔f5 49.♘xh7 ♗g1, Black would still be playing for a win, since the a4-pawn is weak.

45.e3 h5 46.♔e2 h4

What else? Sooner or later Black has to save his bishop.

47.gxh4 ♗xf4 48.exf4 ♔e6 49.♔f2 ♔f5 50.♔g3 ♗e8 51.h5 ♗xh5 52.♘xd5

52...♗e8? After this move Black's problems grow. There was still a simple enough draw after 52...♗f7! 53.♘xb6 ♔e6, going after the knight: 54.♔xg4 ♔d6 55.♘c8+ ♔d7 56.♘a7 ♗b3 57.♘b5 ♗xa4 58.♘c3 ♗b3, and this should be a draw.

53.♘xb6

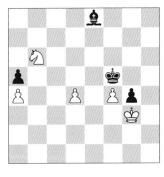

53...♗f7? Finally, the losing mistake. White's tenacity and poker abilities have paid off in full.
Instead, after 53...♗e6 54.♔xg4 ♔d6 55.f5 ♔c6 56.♘c4 ♔d5 57.♘xa5 ♗xa4 58.f6 ♗e8 59.♔f5 ♔xd4, Black would still have got a drawn position.

54.d5 ♗g6 55.♘c4 ♗h5 56.♘xa5 ♗f7 57.♘c4

The pawn is protected via ♘e3+, so Black resigned.

Beating Magnus is a serious feat, especially from a worse endgame.

A lot of heart and tenacity

Beating Magnus is a serious feat, especially from a worse endgame. It takes a lot of heart and a lot of tenacity to keep producing chances when your opponent is one of the best converters in the world.

Magnus Carlsen
Maxime Vachier-Lagrave
Abidjan Blitz 2019 (2)
Sicilian Defence, Najdorf Variation

1.e4 c5 2.♘f3 d6 3.d4 cxd4 4.♘xd4 ♘f6 5.♘c3 a6 6.♗e3 e5 7.♘f3 ♗e7 8.♗c4 0-0 9.0-0 ♗e6 10.♗b3 b5 11.♗g5 ♘bd7 12.♖e1 ♖c8 13.a3 h6

A novelty, although Black has many plausible moves, such as 13...♘b6, which looks quite logical to me.

14.♗xf6 ♘xf6 15.♘d2 ♗g4

Maxime is planning to use the weakened dark squares via this intermediate move. Another logical plan would be to play 15...♕d7, followed by ...♗d8-b6, or, sometimes, ...a5.

16.f3 ♕b6+!? The queen doesn't really belong here, whereas Black's bishop does. The simple 16...♗e6, followed by ...♕d7, was strong.

17.♔h1 ♗e6 18.♘f1 ♖c5

I think it was here that Maxime decided that in a worst-case scenario he would sacrifice the exchange on c3, with a playable position. Although close to the truth, this is not really necessary.

19.♘e3 ♖fc8 20.♖e2 ♖xc3!?

While not brilliant or even especially creative, this sacrifice certainly puts a different spin on the position, since a lack of balance in a blitz game tends to produce more mistakes from both sides.

21.bxc3 ♖xc3 22.♕e1 ♕c6 23.a4 b4 24.♘d1 ♗xb3 25.♘xc3 ♗c4 26.♘d1 ♗xe2 27.♕xe2

The tactical melee has ended in White's favour, although Black is not without chances to equalize and hold the position.

27...d5 28.exd5 ♘xd5 29.♕e4 ♕e6 30.♘e3 ♘c3 31.♕c4

31...♕g6?!

It's scary to trade queens into an endgame an exchange down against Magnus, and Maxime finds ways to

avoid it, even though it entails taking more risks.

After 31...♕xc4 32.♘xc4 f6 33.♘d2 ♔f7 34.♘e4 ♘d5, for example, it's hard to see how White can strengthen his position and open files for the rook to start counting.

32.a5 ♔h7 33.♖e1

33...e4! MVL knows that his chances lie in getting some skin off White's king, so he tries to open access for his knights and bishops to some squares. This also means that White's rook will become more powerful and the objective evaluation of the position will be turning into White's favour. But blitz is blitz.

34.fxe4 ♘xe4

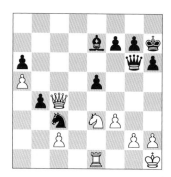

35.♘d5? The gamble has paid off and Black suddenly has real chances. 35.♕d5!, covering the f5-square with the queen and threatening to trade with ♕f5, was far stronger. After 35...♘f2+ 36.♔g1 ♘h3+ 37.♔f1 ♘f4 38.♕f5 White should have a technically winning position.

35...♘f2+ 36.♔g1 ♘h3+ 37.♔f1 ♕f5+ 38.♔e2 ♕e5+ 39.♘e3 ♘f4+ 40.♔f1 ♘e6

The position has become more volatile, and now White has only one move to keep a serious advantage.

41.♕xa6? A strange choice coming from Magnus, because with the loss of the h2-pawn, Black clearly has lots of swindling room.

After the best 41.♘d5 ♕f5+ 42.♔g1 ♗d6 43.♖f1 ♕e5 44.g3 White consolidates his edge.

41...♕xh2 42.♕d3+ ♔g8 43.a6? The mistakes pile up, and Magnus misses Black's actual threat, which is not 43...♘f4, but a nice prep move instead.

43...♗h4! 44.♕d2 ♘f4

The mating net is complete. With 45...♕h1+ coming, Magnus resigned.

As you can see from this game, MVL uses poker tactics of bluffing and increasing his expected equity in the position by finding the kinds of moves that fit the optimum scenario. This is a very smart way to play blitz, even, as it turns out, against the best players in the world.

Never relent

Another remarkable quality that MVL possesses is the ability to continue finding creative ways to get his plan through. In the following game he outplays Hikaru Nakamura in the opening and early middle-game, but stumbles against the American's inventive defence – only to keep looking for winning chances and amazingly succeeding in just under 100 moves.

Maxime Vachier-Lagrave
Hikaru Nakamura
Abidjan Blitz 2019 (3)
Ruy Lopez, Berlin Defence

1.e4 e5 2.♘f3 ♘c6 3.♗b5 ♘f6 4.0-0 ♘xe4 5.d4 ♘d6 6.♗xc6 dxc6 7.dxe5 ♘f5 8.♕xd8+ ♔xd8 9.h3 ♗e8 10.♘c3 h5 11.♗f4 ♗e7 12.♖ad1 ♗e6 13.♘g5 ♖h6 14.♖fe1 ♗b4

This was actually the sixth time that MVL and Nakamura had contested this Berlin Defence position, and while the engines are happily showing 0.00, there is obviously a lot of meat in this position.

15.a3 ♗xc3 16.bxc3 h4 17.♘e4 ♖g6 18.g4 hxg3 19.fxg3

19...♘e7 The first new move is played by Hikaru, who previously drew this position after 19...♗d5 against MVL. 19...♖d8 is also a reasonable alternative.

20.h4 ♘d5 21.♗g5 ♗f5 22.h5 ♘xc3

Complicated tactics have started, in which memory will play an important role. It has been said that MVL's recollection of prep lines is among the very best amongst the elite.

23.hxg6 ♘xd1 24.♔g2

To play a move like this in a blitz game shows that MVL is still deep in his preparation, whereas Hikaru is already on his own.

24...♗xg6?

Here goes: the correct way is 24...fxg6! 25.e6 ♔f8! 26.e7+ ♔f7 27.♖f1 ♔g8 28.♖xd1 ♗xe4+ 29.♔f2 ♖e8 30.♖d7 c5 31.♖xc7 ♗c6 32.♗e3 ♔f7 33.♗xc5 ♔e6, and Black holds. You either know this or you're in trouble. The latter happens to Hikaru now.

25.♘c5 b6 After 25...♗xc2 26.♖h1! f6 27.♖h8+ ♔e7 28.♖xa8 b6! 29.exf6+ gxf6 30.♗h6 bxc5 31.♗f8+ ♔e6 32.♗xc5 White would also have good winning chances.

26.♘a6 ♖c8 27.♖xd1 ♗xc2

Hikaru Nakamura does not look too pleased with his opening, but it would take MVL almost 100 moves to grind down the inventive American.

28.♘xc7+! The key tactic that makes a decisive difference. Now Black's position is objectively lost.

28...♔f8 29.♖d8+

Trusting his technique, MVL simplifies, although logic dictates that keeping the rooks on the board should give him additional chances to play for mate and would therefore be the stronger approach.

29...♖xd8 30.♗xd8 ♗d3 31.♔f3 ♗c4 32.g4 ♗f1 33.g5

Maxime wants to create a passed e-pawn by sacrificing the g-pawn. Black tries to resist.

33...♗d3 34.♔e3 ♗f1

Hikaru decided not to fight the inevitable, since e6 is also a strong plan.

35.g6! ♗h3 36.gxf7 Although this is a logical continuation of White's plan, activating the king, followed by

e6, would probably be stronger.

36...♔xf7 37.♗g5 ♗c8 38.♔d4 ♗d7 39.♔e4 ♗c8 40.♔f4 ♗d7 41.♘a6

Reluctantly White moves the knight, allowing Black's king to activate. What other plan is there?

41...♔e6 42.♔e4 ♗c8 43.♘b4 c5 44.♘a2

Here comes MVL's nifty knight's play.

44...♗b7+ 45.♔f4 b5

Objectively, Black should now be able to save the game, but practically we will see how strong MVL's tenacity in continuing to find chances really is.

46.♘c1 ♔d5 47.♗e7

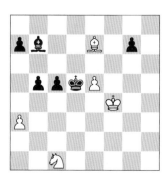

47...a5 Activating the g-pawn was now possible with the unlikely 47...♗c8 48.♘d3 g5+ 49.♗xg5 ♔d4 50.♘c1 b4 51.axb4 cxb4 52.♗e7 ♔c4, with a draw.

48.♘b3 c4

Black finds the plan with ...♗c8 and ...g5, but would have been better off starting with 48...b4.

49.♘xa5 ♗c8 50.♗b4 g5+ 51.♔xg5 ♔xe5 52.♘c6+ ♔e4

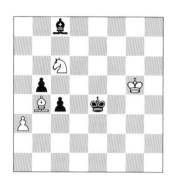

This position could qualify as a study, seeing that White has only one move to give him serious winning chances.

53.♔f6? This is not it! The best restructuring could be had as follows: 53.♗e1! ♗b7 54.♘b4 ♔d4 55.♘a2! ♗d5 56.♘c3 ♔c5 57.♔f4 ♗f7 58.♔e5 ♗h5 59.♗f2+ ♔c6 60.♘d5 ♗f3 61.♘b4+ ♔d7 62.♔d4 ♗d1 63.♔c5 ♗a4 64.♘d5, and White should eventually win.

53...♔d3 54.♘e5+ ♔d4

A somewhat strange decision, since the logical 54...♔c2 should draw easily after 55.♘f3 c3 56.♘d4+ ♔b2 57.♘xb5 c2.

55.♘c6+ ♔d3 56.♔e5 c3 57.♘d4 c2 58.♘b3

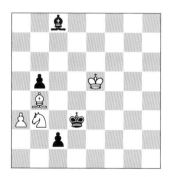

58...♔c4?!

Hikaru is again shy to go to the promotion square.

Black draws after 58...♔e2! 59.♗d2 ♔d3! 60.♗c1 ♔c3 61.♘d4 b4.

59.♘c1!

MVL demonstrated sound endgame play, luring Magnus into a trap, tempting him to overreach.

And suddenly Black is lost, since the king is shut off from coming to the help the c-pawn. 'The rest is a matter of technique', as some crazy people say. I wonder how many GMs could repeat what MVL did over the next 40 moves.

59...♗g4 60.♔f4 ♗h5 61.♔e3 ♗g6 62.♔d2 ♗f5 63.♘e2 ♗g6 64.♔c1 ♗d3 65.♘f4 ♗f5 66.♘g2 ♗g6 67.♘e3+ ♔d4 68.♘g4 ♗f5 69.♘f6 ♔e5 70.♘e8 ♔d5 71.♔b2 ♔c6 72.♘g7 ♗e4 73.♗d2 ♔d6 74.♔c3 ♗g6 75.♔d4 ♔e7 76.♔e5 ♗h7 77.♘e6 ♔d7 78.♘d4 ♗d3 79.♔d5 ♗c4+ 80.♔c5 ♗d3 81.♔b4 ♔d6 82.♔c3!

Picking up the pawn.
82...♗g6 83.♘xb5+ ♔c5 84.a4 ♔b6 85.♔b4 ♔a6 86.a5 ♗e4 87.♘c7+ ♔b7 88.♘e6 ♗f5 89.♘c5+ ♔c6 90.♗e3 ♗h7 91.♘b3 ♔b7 92.♗f4 ♔a6 93.♘c5+ ♔a7 94.♔b5 ♗f5 95.a6 ♗h3 96.♔a5 ♗f1 97.♗e3 ♗e2 98.♘e6+ ♔b8

And Black resigned.
As you can see, MVL's impressive opening preparation, coupled with his great technique, are very strong attributes in blitz.

Beating Magnus again

In his second blitz encounter with Magnus Carlsen in Abidjan, MVL demonstrated sound endgame play, luring Magnus into a trap, tempting him to overreach. This is a common way of playing against really strong players: get them to think they can become active, but don't give them anything to bite on when they get there.

Maxime Vachier-Lagrave
Magnus Carlsen
Abidjan Blitz 2019 (11)

position after 33.♔g2

The players got to this position by playing very sound chess, and although the position is dynamically balanced, there are a lot of tricks that both sides can fall for.

33...♘e5 34.f4 ♘d3

This jump looks like it's moving the knight where the action is, but 34...♘g4, eyeing the h2-pawn and the e3-fork, would actually have been more precise. Then, after 35.♖xa2 ♖xa2 36.♖d8 ♖c2 37.♖d3 e5 38.h3, Black could temporarily shock White with the cute 38...f5!, which leads to a level position after 39.hxg4 fxe4 40.♖d6 e3 41.♔f3 exd2 42.fxe5.

35.♔f1

35...♖a1+?!

Magnus is excited by the prospect of his knight on d3 doing some damage, but Maxim had seen further. It was better to 'keep the position' with 35...♖xc2 36.♖xc2 g5 37.♔e2 ♖d7.

36.♔e2 ♖d7 37.♘f3!

The knight turns out to be somewhat trapped on d3, and it will take some inventive play to avoid problems.

37...♖b1 38.♖d2

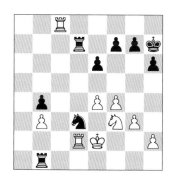

38...♖b2?

The World Champion falls into the trap. The only way to stay alive was 38...♖xb3 39.♘e1 ♘xf4+ 40.gxf4 ♖xd2+ 41.♔xd2 h3 42.♖c7 ♔g8 43.♘d3 ♖xh2+ 44.♔e3 g5 45.fxg5

hxg5 46.♘xb4, when, of course, White would continue trying to win, albeit in a theoretically drawn position.

39.♖xb2 ♘xb2 40.♘e5!

The trap door closes. Remember how I mentioned that Maxime is awesome with the knights?

40...♖d4 41.♔e3?!

Here White could have secured an even bigger advantage with 41.♖c2 ♖xe4+ 42.♔f3 ♖xe5 43.fxe5 ♘d1 44.♖c4, but Maxime decides to go into a winning endgame by picking up some pawns.

41...♘d1 42.♘xf7

42...♖e1+

The alternative was to capture the b-pawn, but White is winning after 42...♖d3+ 43.♔e2 ♖xb3 44.♖h8+ ♔g6 45.♘e5+ ♔f6 46.♖b8 ♔e7 47.♖b7+ ♔d8 48.♖xg7 ♖c3 49.♖b7 b3 50.f5 exf5 51.exf5 ♘c4 52.♘xc4 ♖xc4 53.♖xb3 ♖c2+ 54.♔f3 ♖xh2 55.♖e3.

43.♔d4 ♖e2 44.h4

Even stronger was 44.f5 exf5 45.exf5 g5 46.♖c7.

44...♔g6 45.♘e5+ ♔h5

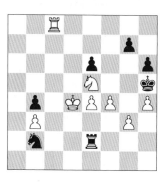

46.♖g8 It's hard to find strong retreating moves in blitz, but after 46.♖c1!, planning ♖b1 or ♖h1, Black is completely paralysed.

46...♖d2+?!

The last hope was to activate the knight. Still, after 46...♘d1 47.♖xg7 ♘f2 48.♘d7 ♘xe4 49.♔d3 ♖e1 50.♘e5 ♘f2+ 51.♔d2 ♖b1 52.♔e3 ♘d1+ 53.♔d4 White should win, provided he avoids the stalemate trick 53...♘e3!? 54.♔xe3 ♖e1+ 55.♔d4 ♖e4+ with 56.♔c5 ♖xe5+ 57.♔xb4.

47.♔e3 ♖c2 48.♖xg7 ♖c3+ 49.♔e2 ♘d1

Black goes for stalemate, but MVL is vigilant enough and spurns the knight, when the rook would happily sacrifice itself next.

50.g4+! ♔xh4 51.♔xd1 ♔g3 52.f5 ♔f4 53.♘g6+ ♔xe4 54.f6 ♖f3 55.f7 Black resigned.

As we have seen in his game against Hikaru Nakamura, once Maxime has a technical advantage, it's very hard to get back into the game against him, because he uses his great speed and persistent aggression to put you onto the defensive, making it very difficult to spot counter-chances. ∎

ARTHUR VAN DE OUDEWEETERING

The thorn in the side

A far advanced rook's pawn can boost your position more than you might think.

L et's start off with David Bronstein's debut in the USSR championship finals, his first round game against Alexander Tolush, played many years before AlphaZero began to show its fascination with advanced rook pawns.

Alexander Tolush
David Bronstein
Moscow 1944

1.d4 ♘f6 2.c4 d6 3.♘c3 e5 4.e3 ♘bd7 5.♘f3 g6 6.♗e2 ♗g7 7.b3 0-0 8.♗b2 ♖e8 9.♕c2 c6 10.0-0 ♕a5 11.♖fd1 ♘f8 12.a3 e4 13.♘d2 ♗f5 14.b4 ♕c7 15.♘f1 d5 16.cxd5 cxd5 17.♕b3 ♖ed8 18.♖dc1 ♕e7 19.a4 h5 20.a5 h4 21.♗a3 21.h3 could be met by ...♗e6, ...♘h5 and ...f7-f5-f4, while Black could also prepare an attack with ...g6-g5-g4.
21...h3 22.g3

22...♘8h7 23.♘d2 ♘g5 In *The Sor-*

cerer's Apprentice Bronstein says: 'The h-pawn creates weaknesses in the position of White's pawns.' He may have been inspired by the famous game Alekhine-Rubinstein, The Hague 1921, which started with 1.d4 d5 2.♘f3 e6 3.c4 a6 4.c5 ♘c6 5.♗f4 ♘ge7 6.♘c3 ♘g6 7.♗e3 b6 8.cxb6 cxb6 9.h4 ♗d6 10.h5 ♘ge7 11.h6 g6. **24.b5 ♕e6 25.♘a4 ♗g4**

A standard idea. With the exchange of the light-squared bishops Black wants to establish an even firmer grip on the weakened squares. **26.♕d1** 26.♗f1 will be met by 26...♗f3, followed by moves like ...♕e6-f5 and ...♘f6-g4, when Black's attack will soon be decisive. **26...♕f5 27.♗e7** At least exchanging one attacking piece (the f6-knight), but this will prove insufficient in the long run. **27...♗xe2 28.♕xe2 ♖dc8 29.♗xf6 ♗xf6 30.♘c5 b6 31.axb6 axb6 32.♖xa8 ♖xa8 33.♘a6 ♗e7 34.♔f1** 34.♖c6 was more resilient.

34...♖c8! This was Bronstein's idea. The a6-knight is misplaced, and despite all the exchanges the white king and the h2-pawn remain in danger. **35.♕d1 ♖xc1 36.♕xc1 ♔g7! 37.♕c7 ♗f6 38.♘b4 ♘f3 39.♘xf3 ♕xf3** You see, the h3-pawn still nailed it! **40.♔e1 ♕h1+ 0-1.**

Here is a more direct king attack along the dark squares based on the daredevil on h6. With the Bronstein example in mind, finding the next virtually winning move here should not be difficult.

Simagin-Nikitin
Kislovodsk 1966
position after 21...g6

22.♗g5! ♗xg5 23.♘xg5 ♕e7 24.♕f4 b3 25.cxb3 ♗xb3 26.♖a1! ♖xa1 After other moves a white rook will support the attack decisively, either from the side: 26...♖xb2 27.♖a6 ♘b4 28.♖a7, or along the c-file: 26...♖fa8 27.♖xa2 ♗xa2 28.♖c1. **27.♖xa1 ♗c4 28.♗h3** 28.♗f1 ♗xf1 29.♔xf1, opening the c-file for White's rook, looks like a straightforward solution. After 29...f6 30.exf6 ♘xf6 31.♘xf6+ ♕xf6 32.♕xf6 ♖xf6

ANALYSIS DIAGRAM

the h6-pawn remains of immense value in this endgame, in which White can choose from various attractive alternatives. You will notice that in similar positions with the rook pawn advanced this far, the other player typically

Had Black sensed the danger he would not have allowed the advance of the enemy rook's pawn.

faces back rank problems and a vulnerable h7-pawn when the endgame approaches. Also, a rook on the 7th file may wreak havoc with the support of the h6-pawn, which in its turn immediately becomes a dangerous advanced passed pawn when the h7-pawn drops. All that being said, 33.♖a6 is most convincing here, e.g. 33...♘d8 34.♖a7, winning. After the text-move, however, Black is also virtually paralysed. **28...♕d8** 28...♖b8 29.♘f6+ ♘xf6 30.exf6 ♕d8 31.♗xe6 fxe6 32.♖a7! is one nice variation. **29.♖a8 ♕e7** 29...♕xa8 30.♘f6+ ♔h8 31.♘xd7. **30.♘f6+ ♘xf6 31.exf6 ♕b4 32.♕c7** If 32...♕e1+ then 33.♔h2 ♕xf2+ 34.♗g2 ♕xf6 35.♖xf8+ ♔xf8 36.♘xh7+ puts an end to Black's resistance. 1-0.

This thorn in your opponent's side may not only severely restrict his king, but sometimes manages – unexpectedly – to bury the fianchettoed bishop!

Zviaginsev-Goganov
Moscow (rapid) 2013
position after 18...♗c8

19.h6! ♗h8 20.♗xe8! Petrosian-Schweber, Stockholm 1962, saw the same exchange, burying the same bishop; the e5-pawn will be unable to move without paying a big price. You can find more buried bishops in *Train Your Chess Pattern Recognition*, and in my column in New In Chess 2015/8. **20...♖xe8 21.♕b3 ♖a6 22.0-0-0 ♕d6 23.♘c4 ♕d8 24.♖hg1 fxe4 25.♘xe4 ♕e7 26.♕b5 ♕f8 27.♘xc5** 27.♘cd6 ♖d8 28.♘xc8 would be another thematic exchange, reducing the number of active black pieces. The text-move is more than sufficient. **27...e4 28.d6 ♖c6 29.d7 ♖d8 30.♖d5 ♕xf2 31.♖gd1 ♗xd7 32.♖xd7 ♖xd7 33.♘xd7 ♖xc4+ 34.♕xc4+** Comes with a check. 1-0

Our last position also features opposite-coloured bishops, but not a buried one. So what could ever happen to Black?

Polugaevsky-Padevsky
Havana Olympiad 1966
position after 23...♗c3

24.h4 ♖c8 25.♔g2 ♖c5 26.♕d3 b5 'Had Black sensed the danger, he would

not have allowed the advance of the enemy rook's pawn, but would himself have played 26...h5.' **27.h5 ♗e5 28.♖xc5 ♕xc5 29.♕f3 ♕c7 30.h6** 'The culmination of White's plan (...); the pawn wedge at h6 creates the preconditions for varying mating threats (...)' – Polugaevsky in *Grandmaster Performance*. **30...♗d6?** Allowing a surprising tactical shot. After other waiting moves, e.g. 30...♕d7, Polu would have prepared the advance of the f-pawn with 31.♕e3.

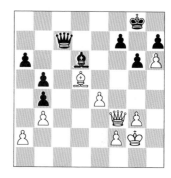

31.e5! ♗xe5 32.♗xf7+ ♕xf7 33.♕a8+ ♕f8 34.♕d5+ ♕f7 35.♕xe5 And even in this queen ending the restricted black king and the vulnerable h7-pawn turn out to be decisive liabilities.

35...♕b7+ 36.♔h2 ♕d7 37.g4 a5 38.♔g3 ♕d3+ 39.f3 ♕d7 40.♔h3 a4 41.♔g3 You can add this zugzwang to Judit Polgar's column in New In Chess 2019/4! **41...♔f7 42.♕g7+ ♔e6 43.♕xd7+ ♔xd7 44.f4** 1-0.

So a little thorn can often have big consequences. Think twice before you allow one. Or, on the positive side, use the thorn to your advantage and restrict your opponent's mobility! ∎

The stars above

There are many ways to improve your play, but studying the stars of our game remains a great recipe. MATTHEW SADLER reviews three new books in which they shine prominently and happily shares his enthusiasm.

Thinkers Publishing has recently published two books in which top-level chess is examined from the perspective of the players who help others become great: the seconds, trainers and captains! The still young (well, compared to me anyway!) French grandmaster and also Guildford teammate Romain Edouard seconded Veselin Topalov from 2010 to 2014, while Ukrainian grandmaster Vladimir Tukmakov – after a long and successful playing career – started a second career as team captain (for the Ukrainian, Azerbaijan and Dutch national teams as well as the SOCAR European Club Cup team) and coach, most notably of two of the world's strongest players: Anish Giri (from 2014 to 2016) and Wesley So (from 2016 to 2017).

As you can imagine, the roles Edouard and Tukmakov fulfilled with their players were somewhat different. Edouard, just 20 years old, was working for a complete player who had done everything there is to do in chess, who was looking for help in generating new creative ideas. As befits a vastly experienced player, Tukmakov's role with Giri and So involved much more mentoring and a steady focus on identifying and eliminating the terrible weaknesses that had restricted them both to mere 2770 ratings! Both Edouard and Tukmakov bring across the peculiar seconds' mix of an agonising sense of responsibility (your player is playing your lines and they have to work against the best players in the world) with a feeling of utter powerlessness as the game unfolds. It's an unusual and very human angle on the games of the world's best players and it makes for gripping reading.

Romain's book *My Magic Years with Topalov* covers Topalov's games from 1995 to the present day, of course with a focus on 2010-2014! Edouard writes that 'although seeing great moves from a 2800 player sounds normal, it was impossible not to be astonished by some of his games'. There are some great players you'd happily steal a few games from for your own Best Games collection and Topalov is definitely in that category for me! Topalov writes in his introduction that 'until Romain told me he was writing it I had no idea of his plans. I believe chess fans will like the honesty of the stories as nothing is hidden' and I can only concur.

A second's life is bound up with both the triumphs and disasters of preparation and this makes this account fascinating as Edouard talks openly both about his pride in great novelties, the pain of seeing great ideas neutralised and the agony of the occasional inevitable disaster. It's also in some ways the story of Edouard's own journey of improvement. As Topalov wittily remarks in his introduction, 'Romain crossed the 2700 benchmark in June 2014; I would like to think it

was because he worked with me, not because he stopped working with me!'

I particularly loved Edouard's account of Topalov's game against Aronian at Wijk aan Zee in 2012. A fairly tame and uninteresting draw that I'd completely ignored is transformed into a fascinating story thanks to Edouard's inside knowledge.

Veselin Topalov
Levon Aronian
Wijk aan Zee 2012

The next game was against Levon Aronian. We played a new idea in the Queen's Gambit, with many dangerous ideas, but Aronian knew it and responded with the best answer.
1.d4 d5 2.c4 e6 3.♘c3 ♗e7 4.♘f3 ♘f6 5.♗f4 0-0 6.a3 b6
The critical answer to 6.a3. We had prepared a relatively new idea against it.
7.♕c2 c5 The first unpleasant surprise. We knew this was the best move! 7...dxc4 was the first move we were hoping for!: 8.e4 ♘c6 9.♖d1 ♘a5 10.♗e2 c6 11.h4 b5 12.♘g5 g6 13.♕c1 We need the white queen in the kingside action! 13...♘b3 14.♕e3

'Although seeing great moves from a 2800 player sounds normal, it was impossible not to be astonished by some of Topalov's games.'

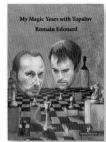

My Magic Years with Topalov
by Romain Edouoard
Thinkers Publishing,
2019
★★★★★

You have to admire White's unshakeable determination to get his pieces pointing towards the kingside! 14...h5 (14...h6 15.♗e5 is difficult for Black) 15.g4 hxg4 16.e5 ♘d5 17.♘xd5 ♕xd5 18.♖g1 c5 19.dxc5 ♕xc5 20.♕e4 ♕c7 21.♘xf7 ♖xf7 22.♖xg4 ♗b7 23.♕xg6+ ♔h8 24.♖d6

and it's game over! 24...♖h7 25.♗h6 Amazing!.

8.♖d1 ♘c6 Another nasty surprise. This move is a powerful equalizer. 8...♗b7 is not as good: 9.cxd5 ♘xd5 10.dxc5 ♕c8 11.♘xd5 ♗xd5 12.e4 ♗b7 13.♖c1 bxc5 14.♗e2 ♕c6 15.♘d2 and we assessed the position as better for White.

9.cxd5 ♘xd5 Now it was clear that Aronian simply knew about our new idea. His preparation was obviously too good, meaning that our whole new idea was spoiled. In general, you hope

to play something new against someone who doesn't know it at all!
10.dxc5 bxc5

This is the whole point. Without preparation one would be afraid of 11.e4 forcing Black to give up his queen, but it simply leads to a very decent position for him. Aronian clearly knew what he was doing, and we had made it clear with Veselin that if this sad situation arose, he should just play a quiet drawish move here, which he did.

11.e3 11.e4 ♘xf4 12.♖xd8 ♖xd8 13.g3 ♘g6 and Black has nice compensation. Levon who likes to 'tease' a bit at press conferences, said something like 'I didn't know anything, but I thought the ending a queen down looks much better for Black'.
11...♕a5 12.♘e5 ♘xe5 13.♗xe5 ♖d8 14.♗d3 ♗a6

and with the following exchanges our lovely, rich preparation fizzles out to a boring, short draw.
15.0-0 ♗xd3 16.♕xd3 ♘xc3 17.♕xc3 ♕xc3 18.♗xc3 ♔f8 19.♖xd8+ ♖xd8 20.♖c1 g6 21.♔f1 ♔e8 22.♔e2 a6 23.g4 ♖d6 24.♗e5 ♖d5 25.f4 f6 26.♗c3 f5 27.h3 ♔d7 28.a4 ½-½.

A collection of great games, inside insights into the play and preparation of one of the world's strongest players and an engaging human story too! What more could you wish for? 5 stars!

■ ■ ■

The focus of Tukmakov's *Coaching the Chess Stars* is slightly different. Obviously, there is still a lot of chess content, but there is also a lot of description of Tukmakov's experiences as a captain and coach. I particularly enjoyed his account of his years as a national team captain for three very different teams as so much of what he wrote resonated with my own experiences in the English national team. The out-of-form players, the moments when players don't want to play, the agonising over board order and team selection, the tensions that lie under the surface when long-time rivals have to work together for one team and that sometimes flare up at the most unexpected moments, and then the glorious moments when – sometimes for no particular discernible reason – it all comes together and a team plays better than you ever dreamt!

I like Tukmakov's writing style a lot: he manages the difficult balance of honesty and openness with a broadly sympathetic treatment of his players. I think this is also due to the fact that he also doesn't spare himself when discussing his own decision-making: he freely acknowledges the doubts he still has about certain choices and is never afraid to own up to his own responsibility for results. Let me just quote some passages, most of which are taken from the end of sections where Tukmakov sums up his experiences, to give you a flavour. For example, on captaining the wonderfully talented Team Azerbaijan:

'It's difficult to assess that period in my career as captain. Team Azerbaijan was unpredictable; I never knew what to expect from these players and in any case, I was unable to understand the team dynamics properly. Exemplary fighting spirit and beautiful victories used to alternate with periods of unexpected underachievement. On the other hand, failure did not necessarily put players in the depths of despair, so revival could occur at any moment. I never managed to understand the logic behind these irregular waves while I worked with the team.'

Then on working with the Dutch team:

'Team chemistry, as people not directly involved in chess understand it, was perfect. There was a nice, friendly atmosphere, mutual help in preparation and joint tea parties. Team spirit gave birth to a "tea spirit". No conflicts or aggression. "We're having fun together!" As long as we played well, relationships within the team were ideal. Even the unavoidable losses couldn't dampen the team spirit. Losses did not force players to try harder next time; on the contrary every loss was perceived as a threat to the players' comfortable existence. Extra exertion often leads to psychological breakdowns, thus the players' motto was "It's not the result that matters but maintaining team spirit". In my opinion, this was the main cause of the stable but fairly unimpressive results by the Netherlands.

'Previous Dutch teams had had a very different experience. Conflicts and quarrels shook those teams to the core and often overflowed. Teammates were not on speaking terms; when something was drunk during team meetings, it wasn't tea. Nevertheless, those teams often won. Even recently, the Netherlands won the European Championship in 2001 and 2005, even though I do not believe

Coaching the Chess Stars by Vladimir Tukmakov
Thinkers Publishing, 2019
★★★★★

that those teams were stronger chesswise than my current one. I do not want to say that it takes conflict within a team to become winners or that good human relationships preclude victories. I am simply pointing out that the absence of true fighting spirit adversely affected several performances of the Dutch national team.'

And finally, a general comment on a captain's role:

'I would venture to advance a subversive argument based on my personal experience. It is not the captain's role to create ideal team chemistry in a national team, and especially not in a club. Players in a team have usually known each other for many years; they are often friendly with each other, but explicit mutual rejection is not uncommon too. It is not practical to waste time and effort trying to patch up something that clearly cannot be fixed. It is wonderful if a team is like a band of brothers! If not, just try to extinguish open fires and focus on chess.'

His account of the collaborations with such players as Kortchnoi and Tseshkovsky as well as Giri and So are just as interesting. Just as with Edouard's account of working with Topalov, the insights of an insider lend colour and interest to games that on the surface might not have grabbed your attention. In summary a really fascinating book that I enjoyed greatly (just as I did Tukmakov's previous books). 5 stars!

Tukmakov manages the difficult balance of honesty and openness with a broadly sympathetic treatment of his players.

One of Tukmakov's coaching experiences was seconding Efim Geller for his ill-fated 1971 Candidates match against Viktor Kortchnoi, an event that also appears in Andy Soltis' *Tal, Petrosian, Spassky and Kortchnoi. A Chess Multibiography with 207 games* (McFarland). This unusual book follows the careers of these four great Russian players from their first steps as juniors, through their greatest moments and often bitter rivalry up to the end of their lives as 'Four Aging Men'. The main part of the book focuses on the period from the late 1950s to the end of the 1960s, when the greatest achievements of three of the players – becoming World Champion – occurred.

I have read many fine biographies of these players, but Soltis' approach brings out something extremely interesting that had not earlier become clear to me. Individual biographies tend to flatten out the peaks and troughs in a player's career. You identify with your hero, naturally cheer the detailed accounts of his successes and then skip quickly past the few pages discussing the odd failure. However, by comparing the players so explicitly to each other and highlighting their interactions with each other, Soltis helps you understand much better the strain and struggles that even these great players faced in chess. You see clearly that when one of them failed, it wasn't just a personal failure, but it probably meant that a bitter rival had succeeded! Soltis highlights how nobody expected that Tal would be the first of these four to attain the goal of World Champion! You can see how Tal's successes influenced the style of others (Spassky most of all), how Spassky stagnated in the early 1960s and how some of these players' most distressing failures were some of the others' greatest successes. Thinking back to Tukmakov's account of the tensions that sometimes exist – and perhaps have to exist – in a national team, I could suddenly see clearly how it all might happen!

Soltis mentions in his introduction that he preferred lesser-known games over the often-published and he makes good on

■ ■ ■

his promise. Just like in Edouard's and Tukmakov's books, the emphasis is not just on the very greatest games that players played but also on revealing the struggles that might not be obvious to the outside observer, so Soltis presents a nice mix of fine games, terrible disasters and bloodless draws to illustrate his narrative. The annotation style is light on variations and very pleasant to read. Let me give you an example from Kortchnoi's 1968 Candidates match with Spassky. In this match, Kortchnoi really struggled with White, losing his first two White games and ending with three losses, one draw and one lucky win with the white pieces. Soltis quotes Spassky as saying frivolously 'In Kiev, where Viktor and I played the final Candidates match in '68, I understood the very first day that I would win. He arrived with his wife, I had two blondes'. Whatever the reason, Spassky played some very good chess in this match!

Viktor Kortchnoi
Boris Spassky
Kiev 1968

1.c4 e6 2.g3 d5 3.♗g2 ♘f6 4.♘f3 ♗e7 5.0-0 0-0 6.b3 b6 7.♗b2 ♗b7 8.e3 c5 9.♕e2 ♘c6 10.♖d1 ♖c8 11.d3 ♕c7 12.♘c3 ♖fd8 13.♘h4 dxc4

This move reveals a sharp difference in positional thinking. Spassky liked to resolve the centre tension this way. Kortchnoi felt it was a basic mistake because it grants White a mobile centre and rules out ...d4. After Nigel Short played 1.♘f3 c5 2.b3 d5 3.e3 ♘f6 4.♗b2 e6 5.c4 dxc4 and beat him

Tal, Petrosian, Spassky and Kortchnoi. A Chess Multibiography with 207 games by Andy Soltis MacFarland, 2019
★★★★★

in a 1996 game, Kortchnoi lectured him: 'You played a match for the World Championship so you should understand the position better.' In any case, computers say 13...d4 favours Black. e.g. 14.♘b5 ♕d7 15.exd4 a6 16.♘a3 cxd4. **14.bxc4 a6 15.♖ab1 ♘a7 16.♗xb7 ♕xb7 17.♘f3 b5**

This was Spassky's aim when he played 13...dxc4. He seeks an outside passed pawn, but grants Kortchnoi a tactical trick, 18.cxb5 axb5 19.♘xb5, based on 19...♕xb5 20.♗xf6 and 19...♘xb5 20.a4. Spassky could have bailed out with 18...♘xb5 19.♘e5 ♘d6, when he would be slightly worse. More likely he would have gone into the unclear 18...axb5 19.♘xb5 ♘xb5 20.a4 ♘d4.

18.♘d2 ♕d7 19.♘de4 Spassky did not think much of Kortchnoi's early knight manoeuvres in this – or in many other games. 'Viktor spends his time in the opening with the White pieces putting them all in the wrong places so that he can reposition them in the early middlegame,' he later told Robert Byrne. 'He's done that all his life. It's his style'. Here Black's superiority would be clear after 19...♘xe4 in view of 20.♘xe4 f5 21.♘c3 b4.

19...b4 20.♘xf6+ ♗xf6 21.♘e4 ♗xb2 22.♖xb2 f5 23.♘g5 ♘c6 24.f4

The trend is running against White. It was time for Kortchnoi to look for tactics. 24.d4 would eliminate his main weakness, the d-pawn. It works because 24...cxd4 25.exd4 ♘xd4 is refuted by 26.♖xd4 ♕xd4 27.♕xe6+ and mates. The position would be in rough balance after 24...h6 25.♘f3 e5 26.♖bd2.

24...e5 25.♕h5 h6 26.♘f3 ♕e6 27.♘xe5 ♘xe5 28.fxe5 ♕xe5 29.♖e2 ♖c6 30.♕f3 ♖cd6 31.♖ed2 Both players missed 31.d4, which Black should have prevented with 30...♖e6. **31...a5 32.♕f4 ♕e6 33.♔f2 a4 34.♔e2 g5**

Kortchnoi later told Garry Kasparov that Spassky's superiority at the time lay in his ability to maintain tension in a position, complicate matters in time trouble and make 'strong, unexpected moves at decisive moments... when I no longer had any time left'. Or as Spassky would say, they met at the summit and only one remained on top.

35.♕f2 ♔g7 36.h4 ♕e5 37.♕f3 ♖e8 38.♔f2 gxh4 39.gxh4 ♖g6 40.♖h1 f4 41.exf4 ♕d4+ 42.♔f1 h5 0-1.

Great stuff! And, all in all, another wonderful book, once again beautifully produced by McFarland! 5 stars. ∎

Jan Timman

A tribute to Pal Benko

His rapid match against Czech promise Thai Dai Van Nguyen did not go as desired, but while in Prague, **JAN TIMMAN** received the news that he had won the endgame study tournament to celebrate the 90th anniversary of the great Pal Benko.

For donkey's years, Pavel Matocha has been organizing two yearly matches in Prague between Czech players and well-known foreign grandmasters. For this year's edition, he had contracted China's number one Ding Liren and myself to take up cudgels against David Navara and the promising junior player Thai Dai Van Nguyen, respectively. The venue was the stately Obecni Dum, the Municipal House on Republic Square in the heart of Prague – an extremely digni-fied location.

It had been difficult for Matocha to find suitable dates, because Ding Liren has a very busy programme. In the end, it was decided to have 10-game rapid matches in three days, wedged between the top tour-naments of Stavanger and Zagreb. There is a question that is exercising many people: had Ding Liren done well or poorly in Stavanger? In clas-

sical chess, he had shared first place with Carlsen after winning prestige duels against Caruana and Mame-dyarov. The Armageddon games, however, had put a spanner in the works, leaving him in sixth place overall. I decided to ask him in Prague what he thought of the idea of those Armageddon games. You'd expect the Chinese grandmaster to condemn it in the sharpest possible terms, but he didn't. He just said that it had not worked very well for him personally. He did add, however, that the Armageddon games might nega-tively affect the next day's classical games, implying that he regarded the classical games as more impor-tant. I completely agree, although I understand the experiment of the Norwegian organizers: you must make concessions if you want to show chess on television.

In Prague, Ding Liren showed that he can also play phenomenally with a faster time-control. He beat Navara

7-3, a first-rate achievement. Ding Liren's play is particularly strong as regards strategy and technique. One example is his final game.

Ding Liren
David Navara
Prague 2019 (10th match game)
Caro-Kann, Exchange Variation

1.e4 c6 2.d4 d5 3.exd5 cxd5 4.♗d3 ♘c6 5.c3 ♘f6 6.h3 g6 7.♘f3 ♗f5 8.♗e2 ♗g7 9.0-0 0-0 10.♗f4 ♘e4 11.♘bd2 f6 12.♘xe4 ♗xe4 13.♘d2 ♗f5 14.♗g3 e5 15.dxe5 fxe5 16.♖e1 ♔h8 17.♘f1

17...d4 Black should have waited with this advance, because it gives White too many squares. Better was 17...♗e6, after which the position is roughly equal.
18.♗f3 White is exerting strong pressure now.
18...♖c8 19.♘d2 ♕b6 20.♕b3 ♕a6 21.♘e4 ♘a5 22.♕a3 dxc3 23.bxc3 ♕b6 24.♖ab1 ♕c7 25.♖b5 b6 26.♘d6!

The crown on White's strategy. Black is forced to settle for a comfortless endgame.

26...♕xc3 27.♕xc3 ♖xc3 28.♘xf5 ♖xf5 29.♖d5

White is a pawn down, but his positional advantage is overwhelming.

29...♖f8 30.♖d7 ♖fc8 31.♖xa7 ♘c6 32.♖b7 ♘d4 33.♗e4 ♖a3 34.♔h2

34...♖xa2

A blunder in a bad position.

35.♖xg7

Of course. White wins material.

35...♔xg7 36.♗xe5+ ♔f8 37.♗xd4 b5 38.f3 b4 39.♖b1 ♖a4 40.♖b3 ♖c4 41.♗b2 ♔e7 42.♔g3 ♔d6 43.♔f2 ♔c5 44.♔e3 ♖a7 45.♗d3 ♖e7+ 46.♔f2 ♖f4 47.♗c1 ♖c4 48.♗xc4 ♔xc4 49.♖e3 ♖a7 50.♗d2 ♖a2 51.♔e2 b3 52.♖c3+ ♔b4 53.♖c2+ ♔a3 54.♖xa2+

Black resigned.

My match was mainly interesting in view of the enormous 50-year age gap. Thai Dai Van's father emigrated from Vietnam in the late 1980s, and built up a successful business in Prague. The 17-year-old Czech is by far the strongest junior player in his country. In the Prague Challengers earlier this year, he did quite well. He has a sharp eye for tactical complications.

In the end, I went under with the same score as Navara. A crucial moment was the end of Game 4.

Ding Liren showed that he can also play phenomenally with a faster time-control.

In Prague, Czech promise Thai Dai Van Nguyen (17) showed his class by beating Jan Timman 7-3 in a rapid match.

Jan Timman
Thai Dai Van Nguyen
Prague 2019 (4th match game)

position after 39...h3

A double-rook ending characterized by an exciting pawn race. I had gone for it thinking that it was a winning endgame. That assessment is correct, but with just three minutes on the clock it's easy to mix things up a bit.

40.♖c8

Obvious, but too direct. White should have dealt with the enemy h-pawn first. This can be done in two ways. First, White has 40.♖e1 h2 41.♖h1 to gain crucial time. Then, after 41... g3, it is time for 42.♖c8, and after 42...♖g1 43.♖xe8 Black is left empty-handed. It is not a difficult line, but in the heat of the battle you can easily choke on it.

More complicated, but also winning was 40.♖e5, with the point of 40...h2 41.♖h5+ ♔g6 42.♖c8 ♔xh5 43.♖xe8. White has a check on h8 up his sleeve.

40...h2

41.♖xe8

After the game Czech grandmaster Jan Smejkal came up to me. We hadn't seen each other for over 20 years. He said I could still

have gone 41.♖e1. That certainly was a better move, but the win was probably already gone. The position contained a spectacular variation that goes as follows: 41.♖e1 ♖g1 42.b8♕ h1♕ 43.♖xg1 ♕f3+! 44.♔c4 ♕e4+ 45.♔b5 ♕d5+ 46.♔b4 ♖xc8 47.♕xc8 ♕d4+, and Black wins back the rook, after which the queen ending is probably just about tenable.
41...h1♕
Now that Black has queened first, he gets sufficient counterplay.
42.♖h8+ ♔xh8 43.b8♕+ ♔h7

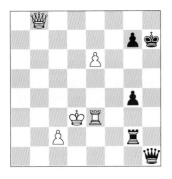

44.♕b5?? A horrible blunder. After 44.e7, 44.♕e5 or 44.c4 a draw would have been inevitable.
44...♕f1+
White resigned. An inglorious end.

■ ■ ■

The highest level of our art
During the tournament I got the happy news from Budapest that I had been awarded first prize in the endgame study tournament to mark Pal Benko's 90th birthday. Not everything had gone against me! The result of the study tournament had been a long time coming because of problems with Benko's eyesight. When someone has reached such a venerable age, you're inclined to worry, but it doesn't seem to be too serious. The problem is of a temporary nature, but he still had to withdraw from judging. He handed the baton to the American study composer Richard Becker, one of the few grandmasters in this field. Becker is known for his strict study criteria. This time, too, only seven of the 65 entries were entered for the award. In his jury report he wrote about Benko: 'His endgame studies are at the highest level of our art. They are filled with novel and counter-intuitive ideas expressed with grandmasterly technique and a degree of economy that truly is pre-computer wizardry'. I agree. In the 1970s, I had several conversations with Benko about endgame studies. He encouraged me to compose more studies, and everything he showed me was fantastic.

This was the reason I had decided to enter one of my very best studies for precisely his jubilee tournament.

Timman 2019
White to play and win
1st Prize Benko 90 JT

White is a rook up, but Black has three potentially dangerous passed pawns.
1.♖d1 A sober starting move. The alternative 1.♖e3+ to take the rook to d3 is insufficient for the win, because it allows the black bishop to cover the d-pawn from the other end of the c1-h6 diagonal. Black sacrifices a pawn to this end: 1...♔g4 2.♖d3 f6! 3.♗xf6 ♗e7! 4.♗a1 ♗g5, and Black has nothing to fear.
1...♗c1 2.♔e2 White must create space for his king.
2...h3 3.♖g1+
Not 3.c4, in view of 3...♔g2 4.c5 ♗a3!

5.c6 ♗d6, and White cannot win.
3...♔h2 If Black withdraws his king to the fourth rank, White will have no problem controlling the passed pawns.
4.♔f2 The end of the foreplay. White has introduced a mating threat. Black, for his part, is going to aim for stalemate.
4...f6 First a pawn sac.
5.♗xf6 ♗b2 And now a bishop sac. The study is approaching its climax.

6.c3!! White makes the same pawn sac, but with totally different intentions. To really understand the position, it is important to check what would have happened after 6.♗xb2. It is clear that Black would need to lose both his a-pawn and his d-pawn. This looks easy enough: 6...d1♘+! 7.♖xd1 a1♕, and if White takes the queen, it is stalemate.

But White still has the fantastic turn 8.♖h1+!. This rook check is known from a slightly different position by the Russian study composer Makletsov. In this situation, it is not enough for the win, however, because after 8...♔xh1 9.♗xa1 h2 10.♔g3 ♔g1 11.♗d4+ ♔h1 12.♗c5 bxc5

Pal Benko celebrated his 90th birthday (15 July 2018) with an endgame study tournament.

13.♔f2 c4 14.b6 c3 the game will still end in stalemate. This is why White needs to shed his c-pawn.
6...♗xc3 7.♗xc3 d1♘+
Black can also reverse the order of queening, which leads to the second main line. It goes as follows: 7...a1♕ 8.♖xa1 (not 8.♗xa1, in view of 8...d1♘+! 9.♔f1 ♘e3+, and it's a draw because the white king must continue to cover the rook) 8...d1♘+ 9.♔f1 ♘xc3, and now the amazing rook sac 10.♖a5!!.

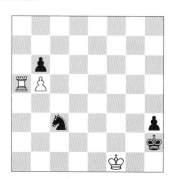

In this position, we have a situation of mutual zugzwang. White to move would be unwinnable, because the rook is tied to the defence of the b-pawn. But it's Black's move. If he takes the rook, the white b-pawn will queen, while 10...♘d5 11.♖a3 will also end up losing – White can cover the b-pawn from b3.
8.♖xd1 a1♕ 9.♖h1+!

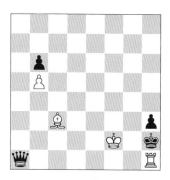

Now Makletsov's rook sac does work.
9...♔xh1 10.♗xa1 h2 11.♔g3 ♔g1 12.♗d4+ ♔h1

13.♗c5!
An echo of the rook sac on a5 in the second main line.
13...bxc5 14.♔f2 c4 15.b6 c3 16.b7 And wins. Because White has sacrificed his c-pawn, the stalemate has been eliminated and Black will be mated. ∎

In the 1970s Benko encouraged me to compose more studies, and everything he showed me was fantastic.

Romain Edouard

CURRENT ELO: 2647

DATE OF BIRTH: November 28, 1990

PLACE OF BIRTH: Poitiers, France

PLACE OF RESIDENCE: Barcelona, Spain

What is your favourite city?
Mine! Barcelona!

What was the last great meal you had?
I can't remember, but surely Japanese!

What drink brings a smile to your face?
A glass of (good) red wine.

Which book would you give to a friend?
One of the books I have written – the one I think might help him most!

What book is currently on your bedside table?
Working at Thinkers Publishing leaves no time for other books at the moment.

What is your all-time favourite movie?
Central do Brasil (1998).

And your favourite TV series?
House is by far my favourite.

Do you have a favourite actor?
Louis de Funès – one of these people who was just born to be an actor!

And a favourite actress?
Perhaps Whoopi Goldberg.

What music do you listen to?
Everything, but in general not recent stuff.

Is there a work of art that moves you?
I would lie if I would name one, although I am very sensitive to art in general.

What is your earliest chess memory?
My classes when I began chess at age five.

Who is your favourite chess player of all time?
Magnus Carlsen. I believe it's the first time we have a World Champion who is better than all his contemporaries in all aspects of the game.

What was your best result ever?
Winning the Dubai Open 2014.

And the best game you played?
Perhaps Edouard-Tkachiev, Belfort 2010.

What was the most exciting chess game you ever saw?
I remember a game Ragger-Moussard from 2014 that was insane.

What is your favourite square?
The one on which I mate.

Do chess players have typical shortcomings?
Chess players, including myself, tend to be in their own world.

What are chess players particularly good at (except for chess)?
Most chess players tend to be good at chess only!

Facebook, Instagram, Snapchat, or?
Only Facebook and Twitter.

How many friends do you have on Facebook?
I think a little more than 2000.

Who do you follow on Twitter?
Friends, chess and tennis.

What is your life motto?
A day only has 24 hours.

When were you happiest?
Probably when I won the U16 European Championship in Herceg Novi, 2006.

Who or what would you like to be if you weren't yourself?
I could make a shortlist of changes I would love to make, but there's nobody else I would wish to be.

Which three people would you like to invite for dinner?
Perhaps three famous politicians (but certainly no extremists), just to understand their thoughts and visions.

What is the best piece of advice you were ever given?
'Make people proud and keep the disappointments inside yourself.'

What would people be surprised to know about you?
I want to keep it a surprise for the day they learn it.

Where is your favourite place in the world?
Definitely the Caribbean – so far.

What is your greatest fear?
Becoming blind!

And your greatest regret?
I always ask myself questions about the past, but I don't really have regrets!

What does it mean to be a chess player?
If you use a chessboard (digital or real) every day or almost every day, you are a chess player!

What is the best thing that was ever said about chess?
Chess is a game for everyone. You can play chess whatever your age, sex, skin colour, religion, handicap...